angles

companion

for Edexcel AS Level

of psychology

Published in 2005 by:
Nelson Thornes Ltd
Delta Place
27 Bath Road
CHELTENHAM
GL53 7TH
United Kingdom

05 06 07 08 09 / 10 9 8 7 6 5 4 3 2 1

A catalogue record for this book is available from the British Library

ISBN 0 7487 8529 9

Illustrations by Angela Lumley, Roger Penwill, David Russell Illustration
Page design and make-up by Michael Fay

Printed in Croatia by Zrinski

Acknowledgements

With thanks to the following for permission to reproduce photographs
and other copyright material in this book:

Albert Bandura: p.44; John Birdsall Social Issues Photo Library: p.58;
Bettman/Corbis: p.38 (left); Corel 184 (NT): p.17; Digital Stock 12 (NT): p.77 (left);
JORVIK: p.18; Alexandra Milgram: p.6; Oxford Scientific Films: p.77 (right);
Photodisc 10 (NT): p.69; Photodisc 17B (NT): p.66 (right); Photodisc 41 (NT): pp.26, 30;
Photodisc 44 (NT): p.66 (left); Rex Features/Garo/Phanie (PHN): p.73;
Dr E. Walker/Science Photo Library: p.19; B.F. Skinner: p.38 (right);
Vin Mag Archive: p.62.

Examination questions in Chapter 8 reproduced with kind permission
of Edexcel Ltd

Picture research by Sue Sharp

Every effort has been made to contact copyright holders
and we apologise if any have been overlooked.

contents

preface   iv

introduction   v
the Edexcel AS specification   v
the Edexcel AS examination   v
general assumptions   vi
research methods   vii
in-depth areas of study   vii
studies in detail   viii
key applications   viii
contemporary issues   ix
evaluating studies and theories   x

unit 1

chapter 1 the social approach   1
what you need to know   2
general assumptions   3
theories of obedience   4
theories of prejudice   5
studies in detail: *Milgram* and *Hofling*   6
research methods: *field experiments* and *surveys*   8
application: *prejudice reduction*   9
contemporary issue: *Internet interaction*   10
questions   11

chapter 2 the cognitive approach   13
what you need to know   14
general assumptions   15
theories of memory   16
theories of forgetting   17
studies in detail: *Craik & Tulving*
and *Aggleton & Waskett*   18
research methods: *experiments* and
case studies of brain-damaged patients   19
application: *eyewitness testimony*   20
contemporary issue: *flashbulb memories*   21
questions   22

chapter 3
the cognitive-developmental approach   25
what you need to know   26
general assumptions   27
Piaget   28
Vygotsky   30
research methods: *observations*
and *longitudinal studies*   32
application: *education*   33
contemporary issue: *computers in education*   34
questions   35

unit 2

chapter 4 the learning approach   37
what you need to know   38
general assumptions   39
classical conditioning   40
operant conditioning   42
social learning theory   44
research methods: *laboratory experiments*
and *animal learning studies*   46
application: *deliberately altering human behaviour*   47
contemporary issue: *media violence*   48
questions   49

chapter 5
the psychodynamic approach   51
what you need to know   52
general assumptions   53
Freud   54
Erikson   59
research methods: *case studies of people in
therapy, clinical interviews* and *analysis of symbols*   60
application: *mental health*   61
contemporary issue: *Buffy*   62
questions   63

chapter 6 the physiological approach   65
what you need to know   66
general assumptions   67
EEGs and sleep stages   68
theories of sleep   69
theory of dreaming   70
research methods: *lesioning, EEG,
brain scanning, twin studies* and *adoption studies*   71
studies in detail: *Dement & Kleitman* and *Heston*   73
circadian rhythms   74
application: *jet lag* and *shiftwork*   75
contemporary issue: *lucid dreaming*   76
questions   77

chapter 7 revision   79
making it work   80
making the best of your time   81
making revision worthwhile   82
making ideas stick   83
improving your exam technique   84
unit 1 revision checklist   85
unit 2 revision checklist   87

chapter 8 examination questions   89
worked examples: unit 1   90
worked examples: unit 2   93
assessment objectives revisited   96

references   97

index   99

preface

The purpose of this book is to guide you through your Edexcel AS Psychology course. Although it will be especially useful at revision time, you will gain more if you use it alongside materials from your lessons and your textbook. The *Angles Companion* follows the layout and examples used in *Angles on Psychology* but it can be used to support any course text. It is intended as a guide, to help you to prepare for the written papers of the AS examination. In order to do this, you need to be aware of what is expected and make the most of what you can learn. This book will help you in both of these ways.

how to use this book

This is not a substitute for attending lessons or reading your textbook. It is designed to reinforce what you know and focus your understanding in order to answer examination questions well.

The text is laid out in boxes so that you can pick out exactly what it is you need to know, check or reinforce. On each page the central idea is often in a central position on the page, you can identify it by its colour – if you are reading a whole spread, start with the darkest box first. This layout means that you can go straight to the box with the information you want. There are also lines to guide your navigation if you want to work through all of the boxes on one topic in a logical order.

Each of chapters 1–6 covers one of the approaches in Units 1 and 2 of Edexcel AS Psychology. They all follow the same format, with an introduction, coverage of general assumptions, followed by a detailed exploration of in-depth areas of study, research methods, studies in detail, key applications and contemporary issues. This is the content that you need to learn. Each chapter ends with two pages of questions. These are similar to examination questions, but not exactly the same. Here you may be asked more specific questions than you could be asked in an examination.

The final chapters offer advice about revision and further opportunities to test your understanding and recall. You can use the question papers to test yourself and then compare your responses to the worked examples of answers given in chapter 8.

acknowledgements

Another huge thank you to the team at Nelson Thornes; especially to Rick, Jess and Nic who have been supportive throughout.

dedication

To the girls of The Queen's School, Chester, who have enthusiastically embraced the idea of this text. Thanks for being such constructive guinea pigs!

introduction

the Edexcel AS specification

The AS Psychology course consists of three units: Unit 1, Unit 2 and Unit 3. Units 1 and 2 are examined on written papers and are the focus of this book. Unit 3 is a single piece of coursework. Within each of Units 1 and 2, three approaches to, or perspectives on, Psychology are covered. The work in each approach follows the same structure:

- two general assumptions;
- two or three research methods;
- several in-depth areas of study (such as theories);
- two studies in detail;
- an application;
- a contemporary issue.

Throughout the following chapters, each of these ideas will be discussed in the same way, with pages devoted to each of the areas listed above.

the Edexcel AS examination

In common with other AS examinations, questions assess candidates' abilities in two skills:

- Assessment Objective 1 (AO1);
- Assessment Objective 2 (AO2).

Assessment Objective 1 (AO1)

- This is a measure of knowledge and understanding.
- It can apply to any part of the specification.
- Clear, effective communication is important.
- It is likely to be measured in questions that ask you to:
  - name, state or identify;
  - define;
  - outline;
  - describe;
  - explain;
  - discuss.

Assessment Objective 2 (AO2)

- This is a measure of the application of knowledge and understanding, analysis, synthesis and evaluation.
- It can apply to any part of the specification.
- Clear, effective communication is important.
- It is likely to be measured in questions that ask you to:
  - discuss;
  - assess;
  - evaluate;
  - criticise;
  - distinguish;
  - apply;
  - compare and/or contrast.

These terms, which you will encounter during your course and in the questions at the end of each chapter, are explained on pages xi–xiii. If you are unsure about any terms, have a look at the revision exercises on page 84.

unit 1

This unit consists of three approaches:

- the social approach;
- the cognitive approach;
- the cognitive-developmental approach.

Unit 1 is examined through one paper lasting 1 hour 30 minutes. It is worth 72 marks, of which 42 marks are for AO1 and 30 are for AO2. The question paper is printed with spaces in which to write your answers. If you run out of room, extra paper will be provided.

Most of the paper consists of fairly short answer questions (1–6 marks) and there is generally one longer question at the end that may carry up to 12 marks. Of these, four are for 'quality of language' – a measure of your spelling, grammar and use of psychological terms. The paper may also contain a small number of questions that, for example, require you to tick or cross boxes, match boxes up with lines or circle correct answers. Questions can include a 'source' – a description of a study, theory or situation that provides the context for testing your understanding. Such sources can give you hints to help you with the question and sometimes it is essential that you refer to this information in your answer – watch out for these questions.

unit 2

This unit consists of three approaches:

- the learning approach;
- the psychodynamic approach;
- the physiological approach.

This is also examined through one paper lasting 1 hour 30 minutes and is worth 72 marks (42 AO1 and 30 AO2). If taken in the same session (e.g. summer) Unit 2 generally immediately follows the Unit 1 paper without a break, so together they feel like a 3-hour examination. The layout of the paper is similar to that of Unit 1.

general assumptions

what are they?

These are central ideas that underpin each approach. You need to learn two per approach and, in general, these are determined by the specification, although in social psychology there is a choice. You could, in addition, learn about further general assumptions beyond those indicated – they are not the only ones.

how are they tested?

Questions on general assumptions are generally for 2 or 3 AO1 marks, so they are asking you to describe or outline an assumption. You could alternatively be asked to relate an assumption to other aspects of the approach or to indicate how an assumption underlies a particular aspect of an approach. Because most of the general assumptions are determined by the specification, you can be asked about particular assumptions stated in the question, for example 'the importance of cognitive abilities' in the cognitive-developmental approach. For example:

- Outline **one** general assumption from the social approach.   [3 marks]

- One general assumption of the psychodynamic approach is the importance of the unconscious mind and motivation. With reference to any material you have learned in the psychodynamic approach (such as theories, studies, methods, applications or contemporary issues) explain how these relate to the general assumption stated above.   [10 marks]

research methods

what are they?

When psychologists conduct investigations they can use a range of different research methods. Some of these are more commonly used in particular approaches than others. For example, longitudinal studies are typical of the cognitive-developmental approach.

how are they tested?

Each research method represents a different way to conduct research and you need to be able to describe each in detail. Questions asking you to do this are worth approximately 2–3 AO1 marks. These methods also have differing advantages and disadvantages (strengths and weaknesses) that you will need to learn. You should then be able to compare different methods in terms of both their characteristics and strengths or weaknesses. Questions may be broken down into parts, asking for description first and then evaluation, or this may be combined into one longer question. For example:

- Describe **one** research method commonly used in the learning approach.
- One method used in the psychodynamic approach is the case study. Evaluate this method in terms of **one** strength and **one** weakness.
- Discuss **two** ways in which field and laboratory experiments differ.

in-depth areas of study

what are they?

In general, this means theories, although in some areas, such as social and physiological, there is additional material to be learned. Theories are ideas that attempt to explain psychological phenomena, such as accounting for why we forget, what dreams are for or how children acquire an understanding of the world. The number of theories per approach varies from two to four. In some approaches (such as cognitive), there is a free choice, in others one or two theories may be determined by the specification.

how are they tested?

Like research methods, questions can ask you to either describe or explain theories or to compare and contrast them. In addition, you can be asked to apply a theory. Questions may be broken down into parts, asking for description first and then evaluation, comparison/contrast or application, or this may be combined into one longer question. For example:

- Describe **one** explanation that accounts for human learning. [5 marks]
- Compare and contrast **two** theories of prejudice. [10 marks]
- Brian's neighbours are very noisy and wake him up at various times during the night. Sometimes he wakes up easily, at other times he seems to sleep through the disturbance. He wonders why, on some occasions, he recalls having been dreaming very vividly but on other occasions has no recollection of dreaming.

  (a) Use your understanding of the stages of sleep to account for Brian's observations. [3 marks]

  (b) Explain how your answer to part (a) could be tested using an EEG. [3 marks]

studies in detail

what are they?

In most cases you will need to know two studies per approach and are free to choose which you learn. In one approach (social), there is a specific study to learn. Generally, it is sensible to choose studies that will help you in other parts of the approach, such as providing evaluation of theories, or evidence for the application or contemporary issue.

how are they tested?

You need to know about the procedure and findings in reasonable detail – for instance, you might learn about the techniques employed and sample used – this will provide for both description of the method and material to evaluate. In general, questions asking you to describe a study are worth 4 or 5 AO1 marks. These are allocated approximately as follows:

- 1 for identifying the study (by a reference – the name of the researchers, e.g. Watson & Rayner – or the 'title' of the study, e.g. 'Little Albert');
- 1 for the aim of the study – what the researchers were trying to find out or test;
- up to 2 for the procedure – how the study was conducted, such as a description of the materials used;
- up to 2 for the findings, e.g. the average of participants' scores in each level of the independent variable (as a number or percentage);
- 1 for the conclusion – what the findings tell us about people in general.

You can also be asked to evaluate a study, generally these questions ask for strengths and weaknesses and are worth 4 AO2 marks. It is important in such questions to remember that you need to express the strengths or weaknesses in relation to that specific study. General points will not gain marks, and each point needs to be written in detail. You could alternatively be asked to describe and evaluate studies in an essay-style question. For example:

- Outline **one** study from the cognitive-developmental approach. [4 marks]
- Describe the procedure and findings of Milgram's study of obedience. [5 marks]
- Evaluate Milgram's study of obedience in terms of both its strengths and weaknesses. [6 marks]

key applications

what are they?

These are real-world situations or issues that can be understood from a particular psychological perspective. There is one per approach and they are all dictated by the specification. Your understanding of an approach should allow you to use concepts, theories and the findings of studies to explain specific aspects of behaviour or cognition. Although you should predominantly be using your existing knowledge of the approach, you are also likely to need to learn some additional material for each key application, for example studies conducted in the field.

how are they tested?

Questions on applications are often essay-style (worth 10 or 12 marks), but they do not have to be. You could be asked to describe an application (for approximately 3 or 4 marks) and then explain it using one or more theory from the approach (this would be worth further marks, about 5 or 6). More difficult questions could ask you to contrast the explanations offered by different theories, for example to distinguish between the advice offered to education by Piaget's ideas and one other theory. For example:

- Describe how jet lag affects circadian rhythms. [4 marks]
- Describe and evaluate **two** ways in which the social approach has offered ideas for reducing prejudice. [12 marks]
- Discuss how concepts from psychodynamic psychology can help to explain mental health issues. [10 marks]

what are they?

Contemporary issues are exactly that, areas of current debate. They may be 'current' because they are problems of today or because they are being actively researched. They are 'issues' because there is an element of debate. When answering questions on a contemporary issue, there are two things you must be clear about. Firstly, it is important to be able to identify why the topic you are describing is *contemporary* – think about the following questions:

- Is it related to current affairs, perhaps trying to understand or explain recent world events?
- Is it at the forefront of psychological research?
- Does it use leading-edge techniques?

Secondly, you need to understand why the topic is an *issue* – try to work out what opinions represent the two sides of the debate. Think about the following questions:

- Can you ask a question about the topic to which the answer might be both 'yes' and 'no'?
- Are there studies that support the opposing viewpoints?
- Are there theories that explain the issue in different ways?

When trying to understand a contemporary issue, remember that you need to employ at least one theory (probably more than one) from that psychological approach. This, in fact, saves you work – if you already understand the theory(ies), then all you need to do is apply them to the issue.

You may be able to utilise studies that you have learned for the approach but beware of simply writing 'everything you know about …'. The evidence you use must help to *explain* the issue.

how are they tested?

Questions on contemporary issues are often essay-style (worth 10 or 12 marks), but they do not have to be. You could be asked to describe a contemporary issue (for approximately 3 marks) and then explain it using one or more theory from the approach (this would be worth further marks, about 5 or 6).

Alternatively, you could be presented with a contemporary issue that you have not encountered before. You could be expected to identify why it is an issue and to explain it using theories from the approach. For example:

- Use your knowledge of the learning approach to discuss **one** contemporary issue or debate. [12 marks]

- 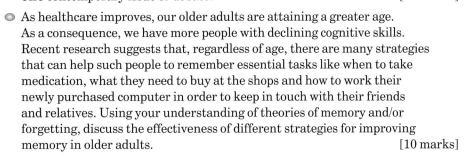 As healthcare improves, our older adults are attaining a greater age. As a consequence, we have more people with declining cognitive skills. Recent research suggests that, regardless of age, there are many strategies that can help such people to remember essential tasks like when to take medication, what they need to buy at the shops and how to work their newly purchased computer in order to keep in touch with their friends and relatives. Using your understanding of theories of memory and/or forgetting, discuss the effectiveness of different strategies for improving memory in older adults. [10 marks]

evaluating studies and theories

evaluating studies and theories

Of the two skills required for AS level, AO2 is probably harder. In order to gain AO1 marks you need to learn the material well, but to gain AO2 marks you must be able to explore and use what you know. One way to do this is through evaluation. The next two sections will help you to engage in that process each time you encounter new ideas.

evaluating studies

Approximately 40% of the marks at AS are for AO2, this is a measure of your ability to:

- **illustrate** your understanding (give examples of);
- **analyse** (justify, give reasons for, explain);
- **synthesise** (pull ideas together, find links between);
- **evaluate** (find **strengths** and **weaknesses**, **criticise**);
- **apply your knowledge** (use it to understand real-life situations or events).

A common way that AS questions ask for AO2 is by looking for an answer that requires you to *evaluate a study*. It is most likely to be one that you have chosen (one of your two from each approach,) although it could be Milgram's study or one that is described to you on the exam paper.

When you evaluate a study you look for its *strengths* and *weaknesses*. Remember, you must consider these *in relation to the particular study*, not just as advantages and disadvantages of different methods or approaches.

approach	identify the studies you will learn for each approach
unit 1	
cognitive	
social	Milgram
cognitive development	
unit 2	
physiological	
psychodynamic	
learning	

You must be able to produce an evaluation for each of these. It should consist of **at least** two strengths and two weaknesses (more for Milgram). Each evaluation point should consist of two parts, for example:

- Study X was good because there was a large sample of 550 people.
  This is a strength because the results are more likely to be representative of the general population so the results can be generalised more widely.
- A weakness of study Z is that it was conducted in a laboratory.
  This is a problem because it was about helping behaviour and people might feel obliged to be helpful in a lab whereas they might not out in the street.

It is essential that each strength or weakness is relevant to that study in particular and is not a general point that could apply to any study.

Lab and field studies of helping behaviour!

Ask yourself these questions whenever you meet a new study

1 Was the study well designed so that it produced valid and reliable results?

(a) Where was it conducted (laboratory or field)?

- Laboratory studies are easier to control and therefore may produce more valid data because in artificial environments there are fewer situational variables that could disrupt the effect of the IV or measurement of the DV. They are generally more reliable as they are easier to replicate.

- Field experiments may be more valid as participants may be unaware of demand characteristics so their behaviour is only affected by the IV not their expectations, but they are harder to replicate as the natural environment can change.

(b) Was the task realistic?

- A realistic task is more likely to produce responses that tell us about real behaviour.

- Artificial tasks may be easier to set up, control and measure the responses to, so they may produce more valid data as the researcher can be more certain about which variables are responsible for changes in participants' behaviour.

(c) Was the participant design appropriate?

- Repeated measures or matched pairs could benefit from low participant variables.

- Independent groups could benefit from fewer order effects or problems with demand characteristics.

(d) Were the participants a representative sample?

- A large sample is more likely to reflect the range of individuals in the target population than a small one.

- Did the sample contain both males and females and people of different ages, ethnic groups, etc? Or, if the findings are only intended to apply to one group (e.g. women's attitudes to pregnancy), was the sample appropriate?

- Consider why students aren't representative – they are fine in a study looking at students' attitudes to increased tuition fees!

2 Do you think the study was conducted ethically?

Consider whether participants:

- were asked for their consent;

- had enough facts to give informed consent;

- were deceived during the study;

- could have been physically harmed by the procedure:
  - Could there have been long-term effects?
  - Were any risks greater than *they would normally have experienced?*

- could have been psychologically harmed by the procedure:
  - Could participants have felt distressed or embarrassed?
  - If so, were they adequately debriefed to restore their emotional state?
  - Was there privacy during the study and confidentiality of results?
  - Did they need to be followed up later, and were they?

3 Are the findings of the study socially sensitive?

- Could the findings cause offence to a group of people in society?

- Could the findings be (mis)used to harm individuals or groups?

- Do the findings tell us something unpleasant about human nature?

4 Is there other evidence that agrees or conflicts with the findings of this study?

- Similar studies could confirm or refute the findings.

- Theories could explain the findings or be supported by them or, alternatively, could contradict the findings or be contradicted by them.

evaluating theories

Questions about theories, like ones on studies, can ask you to:

- **illustrate**;
- **analyse**;
- **synthesise**;
- **evaluate**;
- **apply**.

A common way that questions ask for AO2 is by requiring you to *evaluate a theory*. Some of the theories are dictated by the specification, others I have chosen for you, although you may have studied different ones. If so, try to use the ideas here to help you. In addition, you need to be able to evaluate some ideas (see the table below).

When you evaluate a theory, you look for its *strengths* and *weaknesses* and these must be *in relation to that particular theory*. Also it is not enough to say that it 'explains so-and-so', this will not earn you marks, it's what the examiners call 'explaining what it's supposed to explain' – it would be like saying 'My bike is excellent because the wheels go round when I pedal', well … er … yes … they would, it's a bike. On the other hand, you could say your bike is good because it's better than other bikes (goes faster, etc.) or that it's useful because it can pull a little cart with a dog in it which other bikes can't do.

Avoid trying to evaluate a theory by saying that it 'explains what it is supposed to explain'

approach	identify the theories you will learn for each approach
unit 1	
cognitive	⚬
	⚬
	⚬
	⚬
social	⚬ Milgram's agency theory
	⚬
	⚬ social identity theory
	⚬
cognitive development	⚬ Piaget
	⚬
unit 2	
physiological	⚬ circadian rythms
	⚬ stages of sleep
	⚬ restorational theory of sleep
	⚬
	⚬
psychodynamic	⚬ Freud: psychosexual stages, personality
	⚬ Freud: defence mechanisms
	⚬ Freud: dream theory
	⚬
learning	⚬ classical conditioning
	⚬ operant conditioning
	⚬ social learning theory

You must be able to produce an evaluation for each of these. It should consist of **at least** two strengths and two weaknesses. Each evaluation point should consist of two parts – link the sentences with *so, as, because, however, although*, etc.

It is essential that each strength or weakness is relevant to that theory in particular and is not a general point that could apply to any theory.

Ask yourself these questions whenever you meet a new theory

1 Is the theory testable?

- Some theories are *difficult* or impossible to test (the safe bet is to always say the former). It is a *weakness* if it cannot be tested.
- Some theories can be tested using more effective methods than others – bear in mind that some methods are much more appropriate for testing some theories, it's not just a matter of which method is 'best'. If you are commenting on the advantages and disadvantages of different sources of evidence do so:
  - *in relation to the theory* you are discussing, not in isolation (it's not a research methods question);
  - by comparison with other methods that may or may not be used to test *that theory*.

2 Is the theory supported by evidence?

- Give examples of studies that *support* the theory for strengths (or ones that *conflict* with it for weaknesses) *and* say how or why they support or refute the ideas.
- Consider whether the evidence you have cited is *good* evidence – is it valid and reliable? – if the evidence isn't good then can it really be used to confirm or deny the value of the theory? (See point 1 above.)

3 Is the theory complete?

- If there is something important that the theory *cannot explain*, this is a *weakness*.
- Are there aspects of the particular emotion, cognition or behaviour that the theory attempts to explain which it cannot account for?
- You can compare the efficacy of this theory with other theories.
- You cannot, however, expect theories to explain things that they didn't attempt to explain in the first place!

4 Are there implications of the theory that are socially sensitive?

- Could the ideas cause offence to a group of people in society?
- Could the ideas be (mis)used to harm individuals or groups?
- Does it deal with a topic that people would rather not consider or suggest how people *ought to* behave or think?

5 Does the theory have useful applications?

- Can the theory be used to understand people in the real world so that lives can be improved?
- Explain exactly *what* the theory helps us to understand and *how* it can lead to beneficial changes.

Any evaluation points you write should consist of two parts, for example:

- A strength of theory Z is that it has a lot of supporting evidence, *for example, Bloggs et al. (2005) found that … which shows that Z does cause behaviour A.*

- Theory X can be criticised because it cannot be tested effectively as the definition of X is circular. *This means that valid studies cannot be conducted to demonstrate that A is responsible for B; it is possible that both A and B are caused by another factor.*

chapter 1
the social approach

what you need to know   2

general assumptions   3

theories of obedience   4

theories of prejudice   5

studies in detail   6

research methods   8

application   9

contemporary issue   10

questions   11

the social approach

Social psychology looks at the effect that people, either individually or in groups, have on other individuals and groups. This may change emotions (affect), behaviour or cognitions (think ABC).

what's it about?

general assumptions

You need to understand and be able to describe at least **two** general assumptions of the social approach, e.g.

- the influence of **individuals** – such as obedience to an authority figure;
- the influence of **groups** – such as social identification by football fans;
- the influence of **society** – such as social comparison leading to racism;
- the influence of **culture** – such as the effect of stereotypical language on homophobia.

theories

in-depth areas of study

You need to be able to describe and evaluate:

- **two** theories of obedience:
  - **Milgram's agency theory**;
  - one other, e.g. **charismatic leadership**);
- **two** theories of prejudice:
  - **social identity theory**;
  - one other, e.g. **discursive theory**.

You will also need to be able to apply these theories to situations for the key application and contemporary issue.

classic research *research now*

studies in detail

You need to be able to identify, describe and evaluate in detail **two** studies from the social approach:

- **Milgram (1963)** – the study about 'teacher' participants obeying orders to give apparently fatal electric shocks to a (confederate) 'learner'. Make sure that you can separate what happened in Milgram's *first* and subsequent studies;
- one other study, e.g. **Hofling et al. (1966)** – the hospital field experiment about whether nurses would obey a doctor's instructions about a drug even though they knew they shouldn't.

The second study could be about prejudice.

research methods

methods

You need to be able to outline and discuss research methods commonly used in the social approach including:

- **field experiments;**
- **surveys.**

It is helpful if you can also:

- remember an example of each of these methods being used in social psychology (e.g. Hofling and Poppe & Linssen respectively);
- recognise the differences between field and laboratory experiments.

real lives

key application

You need to understand and be able to discuss links between social theories and strategies for reducing prejudice.

To do this you need to be able to:

- explain how each theory leads to ideas for reducing prejudice;
- describe and evaluate evidence suggesting that these strategies should work;
- discuss how effective the strategies actually are.

You will need to know additional material relating to techniques such as equal status contact, co-operation, collective action and politically correct language.

talking point

contemporary issue

You will need to use your knowledge of the social approach to explain a current issue, e.g. **Internet interaction**.

For this you will need to:

- be able to describe the issue;
- use **at least one concept** from the social approach to explain the issue (e.g. one or more theory of prejudice);
- use terminology from the social approach.

You can also be asked to apply the concepts to a contemporary issue you have *not* studied.

the influence of individuals

how can one individual influence the behaviour, emotions or cognitions of other individuals?

- Sometimes we alter our behaviour because we are told what to do, such as when a car park marshal says 'Park over there'. This is a case of obedience, because we are following the orders of an individual.
- The social approach provides an explanation of this through agency theory which says we learn to act in the best interests of society, so we follow orders from people in authority.
- Some individuals are more likely to influence us than others. For example, if we find someone particularly funny or friendly, we are influenced by them because they are charismatic.

the influence of groups

how can a group influence the behaviour, emotions or cognitions of its members, or of other individuals that are not part of the group?

- We think of people as belonging to groups and respond to those in our group differently from others because they are the 'in-group'.
- As a result we may also have different feelings towards members of our own group and to those who are not, i.e. who are part of the 'out-group', e.g. being frightened or resentful of them.
- This can affect our behaviour, e.g. we show favouritism to people in our own group and may discriminate against the 'out-group'.

the influence of culture

how can culture influence people's behaviour, emotions or cognitions?

- Within a culture we have expectations about the behaviour of other people. As a result there are cultural differences in the influence people can have on one another. For example, in replications of Milgram's study around the world, differing rates of obedience have been recorded.
- Our culture can also subtly affect the way we think or act, e.g. influencing the way we use and understand language.

exam notes

Social: you only have to learn two general assumptions for the social approach, although three are described here.

General: by the end of each approach, you should be able to elaborate the general assumptions with real-life examples as well as relevant studies and theories.

strengths of agency theory

- Evidence from lab experiments (e.g. Milgram) and field experiments (e.g. Hofling) – see page 7 – suggests that people obey authority figures.
- Blass (1996) found that less onus is placed on people when following orders, suggesting we can identify the agentic state in others.
- Knowing the effect of authority figures has practical applications, e.g. to dissuade service men and women from following orders without question so reducing the possibility of wartime human rights abuses or for positive outcomes in the community.

agency theory

Milgram (1974) suggested that social rules are needed to maintain a stable society and that in order to follow them we surrender some of our free will. He proposed that to do this we have evolved two states:

- *autonomous state* – we act as we wish to, according to our own free will or conscience;
- *agentic state* – we give up our free will and act on behalf of the wider group.

During childhood, we are socialised to develop the capacity to enter an agentic state, i.e. to relinquish our own wishes and act in the best interests of our society. One way we do this is by following orders from people in authority within the society. By acting as an agent of these authority figures, we can use defence mechanisms (see page 56) to avoid *moral strain*, the distress of acting in a way we would normally find unacceptable.

weaknesses of agency theory

- The agentic state is difficult to identify because it cannot be defined independently from obedience – the argument is circular. People are said to obey because they are in the agentic state, whilst, conversely, the agentic state is defined by obedience.
- Agency theory cannot explain the effects of personality on obedience – some people are less likely to follow orders (some disobeyed Milgram) and some individuals are more likely to make others obey them even when they are no different in level of authority.

obedience

The tendency to follow orders given by an authority figure

strengths of charismatic leadership

- Evidence supports the role of specific social processes suggesting that leaders who can induce obedience do share characteristic communication styles. Berson et al. (2001) found that charismatic leaders had a clear vision, Chernulnik et al. (2001) showed that US presidents who smiled and held gaze gained greater emotional responses in listeners and Geyer & Steyrer (1998) found charismatic bank managers had more productive teams.
- It has useful applications, e.g. for training political leaders with skills of charisma to increase their effectiveness.

charismatic leadership

House et al. (1991) said charismatic leaders can effectively influence the behaviour of others, e.g. to encourage them to obey orders. Factors that affect a leader's capacity to obtain obedience are:

- *personal characteristics* – a high level of: communication skills, concern for the needs of 'followers' and impression management (portraying an image of yourself you believe others want to see);
- *social processes* – a clear vision of goals and how to reach them, framing orders in the context of these goals and using emotive language to provoke action rather than reflection.

weaknesses of charismatic leadership

- People will obey non-charismatic individuals (e.g. the 'doctors' in Hofling's study) so other factors must affect the tendency to obey.
- Those leaders who are effective do not seem to have consistent personal characteristics suggesting that the effects of charismatic leadership are not the result of a particular personality type.

Are charismatic teachers more likely to gain the obedience of their class?

strengths of social identity theory

- Evidence from minimal groups studies (e.g. Tajfel, 1970) suggests that categorisation, even when it has a limited basis, can cause identification and comparison resulting in discrimination.

- Non-experimental evidence, e.g. from surveys (Poppe & Linssen, 1999) suggests that in-group favouritism (negative social comparison of other groups) occurs when people categorise themselves by nationality.

- It has applications for prejudice reduction (see page 9).

social identity theory (SIT)

Tajfel & Turner (1979) suggested that prejudice arises because we tend to separate people into 'us and them', i.e. members of the 'in-group' or 'out-group'. The three processes we use to make these judgements are:

- *social categorisation* – to which group does this person belong?

- *social identification* – I belong to this group so will adopt its attitudes and behaviours to distinguish myself from non-members;

- *social comparison* – in- and out-groups are measured against each other, the out-group is devalued and the self-esteem of in-group members is raised.

weaknesses of social identity theory

- Further evidence from minimal groups studies has shown that other factors, e.g. having to justify decisions, and group size, affect prejudice (Dobbs & Crano, 2001). This suggests that prejudice is not only affected by categorisation, identification and comparison.

- SIT cannot account for the individual differences that arise in prejudice. For example, Platow et al. (1990) found that people who were more competitive also demonstrated greater in-group favouritism.

prejudice

Prejudice is the holding of an opinion about someone before getting to know him/her as an individual, which is based on stereotypes about the group to which they belong.

There are three elements to prejudice:

- *affective* – feelings/emotions, e.g. hate, anger, disgust, fear;

- *behavioural* – actions towards the target of prejudice (discrimination), e.g. avoidance, verbal or physical aggression, murder;

- *cognitive* – beliefs about the group, e.g. incapable, dangerous, lazy, evil.

strengths of discursive theory

- Evidence (e.g. Burns, 1998 and Parker, 1999) supports discursive theory by showing that prejudice exists in popular language that can account for socially constructed stereotypes.

- It is based on real-world evidence (rather than lab experiments) that provides information which is inaccessible other than through discourse analysis.

- Practical benefits, e.g. the use of politically correct language (such as 'a person with a disability'), can minimise the social construction of prejudiced views.

discursive theory

This says that prejudice arises from the way language depicts groups because this affects our perception of them. The words used in relation to particular groups may cause us to socially construct (i.e. create) artificial differences between people. For example, using 'Blacks', 'gays' or 'the disabled' suggests such individuals are nothing more than their skin colour, sexual orientation or disability, making them seem different from everyone else and not 'people' at all. Also, terms such as 'black' and 'gay' are attributed negative associations, such as 'black mark' or using 'gay' as an insult.

weaknesses of discursive theory

- Attitudes may not be the result of exposure to stereotyped discourse; conclusive experimental studies that allow testing of cause and effect cannot be conducted as exposure to language cannot be controlled.

- Evidence from discourse analysis, a key source of support for discursive theory, is subjective. Researchers may have preconceptions about what they expect to find when they analyse media and consequently are more likely to produce results that support their beliefs about the influence of language.

strengths of Milgram

methodology

controls:

- To increase *validity*, deception ensured that participants believed the situation was real, e.g. being assigned to the role of 'learner' by an apparently random procedure, the apparatus looked authentic and receiving a test shock.

- The verbal prods given to participants were fixed, so that each person received the same orders, increasing reliability.

operationalisation:

- Obedience was operationalised by measuring the voltage reached by each participant.

ethics

- Participants were told that they could leave at any time. Therefore they were initially made aware of their *right to withdraw*.

- Participants received a thorough *debrief* – a detailed account of the study – ensuring that they were returned to their previous state.

- A follow-up questionnaire returned by 92% of the participants showed that 84% were happy to have taken part, so for most participants there were no long-term negative effects.

- They met Mr Wallace after the study to confirm that he was unharmed.

- Milgram had asked colleagues what they expected to happen but the extent of obedience was not foreseen.

- These steps were taken in consideration of participants' welfare even though there were no formal ethical guidelines at the time – these are all aspects of good *conduct*.

Milgram (1963)

Aim: to test obedience to authority – to find out whether 'Germans are different' in an attempt to understand the atrocities of the Second World War.

Procedure: he advertised for volunteers for a study into the effects of punishment on memory. The real participant (the 'teacher') was asked to give electric shocks to another individual (Mr Wallace – the 'learner') who they believed to be another participant but who was, in fact, a confederate. The participant was to increase the shock level each time the learner incorrectly answered the task. No shocks (other than one given to the real participant to illustrate the equipment) were actually administered. The learner began to indicate distress, but if the participants refused to give a shock they were ordered to continue by the experimenter (the authority figure) who had a series of verbal prods to follow. Participants were fully debriefed and were followed up a year later.

Findings: 100% of the participants gave shocks up to 300V, 65% up to 450V.

Conclusion: the high percentage of individuals obeying the instructions suggest that obedience is due to the situation – the perceived authority – not the personality of the participant.

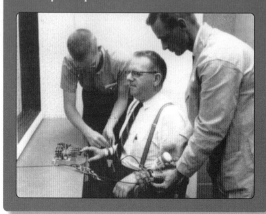

weaknesses of Milgram

methodology

- The initial sample was narrow – 40 male respondents to an advertisement – so the findings could not be *generalised* to the wider population.

- As a measure of obedience, the study lacks *validity* as people would not generally expect to give electric shocks to others.

- If the participants' behaviour resulted not from obedience but from an acceptance that the experimenter was engaging them in a 'trick', the study would have lacked validity. This is, however, unlikely given their distress.

ethics

- Participants were *deceived* about the allocation of learner and teacher roles and about the reality of the shocks.

- Verbal prods put them under pressure so caused *distress*, bringing the *conduct* of the study into question.

- Participants were initially told that they could leave at any time but this *right to withdraw* was denied by the use of verbal prods.

- Participants were invited to a study on memory but it was in fact a test of obedience so they could not give *informed consent*.

variations on Milgram's procedure

Setting: The study was conducted in a run-down office block instead of at a prestigious university.

- Obedience to administering a 450 volt shock fell to 47.5%.
- This suggests that factors contributing to the apparent level of authority of the experimenter affect obedience.

Telephone orders: Orders were given by the experimenter on the telephone from another room.

- Obedience to administering a 450 volt shock fell to 20.5%.
- This suggests that the presence of the authority figure has a direct effect on obedience.

Personal involvement: The 'teacher' was required to hold the learner's hand on an electrode.

- Obedience to administering a 450 volt shock fell to 30%.
- This suggests that obedience can be affected not only by factors relating to the authority figure, but also by factors influencing empathy – when the learner's suffering is harder to deny, obedience is reduced.

These findings show that a range of factors are involved in obedience to authority, even in relatively artificial laboratory situations.

Recent studies of obedience

What factors affect nurses' obedience to doctors?

Krackow & Blass (1995) interviewed nurses about their obedience to doctors and found they tended to obey because they saw doctors as legitimate authority figures. However, they were more likely to challenge orders they believed would have serious consequences for patients.

Is obedience good for pilots?

Tarnow (2000) found that air accidents often occurred when pilots followed orders from the ground even when these came from individuals who were less informed than themselves.

strengths of Hofling

- The study was conducted in a natural environment so the nurses are unlikely to have been affected by demand characteristics as they probably did not know they were participants in an experiment.
- By interviewing the nurses after the experiment, it was possible to establish whether they were aware of the breach of regulations, showing that they knew they were potentially putting patients in danger.

Hofling et al. (1966): doctors and nurses study

Aim: to test whether nurses would obey the instructions of a doctor that breached hospital regulations.

Procedure: nurses on hospital wards were telephoned by an unknown doctor and instructed to give an unknown drug to a patient (at a dosage twice that recommended on the bottle). Separately, 22 nurses were interviewed to find out whether they would administer a drug in the circumstances described above.

Findings: 21 of the 22 nurses asked by telephone to administer the drug did so, but only one of the 22 interviewed said that they would. Of those who did administer the drug, 10 had noticed the discrepancy in dosage but judged that it would be safe as they had been told to do so.

Conclusion: nurses believe that they would not unquestioningly obey doctors' orders, but the majority are likely to do so even when this contravenes rules or their own judgement.

weaknesses of Hofling

- Precisely because telephone orders are risky, they are not allowed. Hence the situation does not replicate a real-life situation. So, even though it was in a natural setting, the study did not have high ecological validity.
- When ecological validity is higher (the drug is familiar and nurses can consult with colleagues), obedience levels fall (Rank & Jacobsen, 1975).
- As the nurses on the ward were unaware that they were taking part in an experiment, there are ethical issues – they could not have given their consent and the effect of receiving and responding to an order that was in breach of regulations may have distressed them. This may have affected their care for other patients.

strengths of field experiments

- As participants are in their normal environment, they may be less affected by the situation than if they were in a laboratory. So their behaviour may be more representative of real life.

- Participants are less likely to be aware that they are in an experiment than those in laboratory studies, so are affected less by demand characteristics, again suggesting their behaviour would reflect the real world better.

- Field experiments *may* be ecologically valid because of the situation (but this is not necessarily the case).

- If participants are unaware that they are in an experiment, there is no need (unlike in some laboratory experiments) to actively deceive them about the study's aims.

field experiments

- Take place in the participants' normal environment, e.g. at college or work, or in the home.

- Have an independent variable (IV) and a dependent variable (DV).

- Predict that the IV will have a causal effect on the DV.

- The IV may be contrived (such as different lighting conditions at work) or, in a natural experiment, naturally occurring (such as different weather conditions).

weaknesses of field experiments

- Participants are unlikely to know they are in a study, which raises the ethical question of deception and consent – they cannot have agreed to participate.

- Because the experiment is conducted in a real-world setting, variables are harder to control than in a lab so there is a greater risk that changes in the DV are the result of extraneous variables. The validity of the findings is thus reduced.

- Because there are fewer controls than in a lab, field experiments are harder to replicate so reliability is lower.

- Contrived field experiments may lack ecological validity because the task or situation is not one that the participants would actually encounter.

strengths of surveys

- Large amounts of data can be collected by asking many questions or many people. Therefore the findings will be more representative than from studies using smaller samples.

- When closed questions are used, the results are easy to collate, score and compare.

- When open questions are used, detailed data can be obtained, giving insight into the reasons for people's attitudes or behaviour and information that it is difficult to obtain through direct observation, e.g. feelings, can be accessed.

- Standardised techniques are used (such as closed questions) so that results are highly reliable and replicable.

surveys

- Large-scale data collection.

- Use questionnaire or interview techniques.

- Can investigate people's attitudes, beliefs or intentions.

- Can use a range of questioning techniques to produce different kinds of data, such as open and closed questions.

weaknesses of surveys

- Closed questions lack flexibility because they do not allow participants to say exactly what they mean. As a result important information may be lost and results may not truly reflect opinions or feelings.

- Responses may be affected by social desirability so participants may respond in the way that they think people ought to, thus reducing the validity of the findings.

- Responses may also be affected by response bias – participants may respond in a set way or may give the answers they believe will help the researcher.

- People's attitudes (as expressed in a survey) are not necessarily good indicators of their behaviour, so the findings of surveys may not be valid predictors of future behaviour.

- Unlike observations, surveys cannot be used with children or animals (with no language).

- Sampling biases may arise if only very similar people are interviewed or return questionnaires.

prejudice reduction: what role can psychologists play?

- By understanding the factors that influence the formation and maintenance of prejudice, it should be possible to identify ways to reduce prejudice.
- Recognising that people's stereotyped beliefs (the cognitive component) and their discriminatory responses (the behavioural component) may be affected independently allows psychologists to tackle both aspects of prejudice.

discursive theory and prejudice reduction

The discursive theory suggests that prejudice arises because language can convey underlying – and prejudiced – social constructs. As a result, members of a society can be affected by discriminatory language; acquiring stereotyped beliefs without having been exposed to the targets of their prejudice at all.

This suggests that prejudice may be tackled by reducing the use of discriminatory language.

inter-group contact

Contact between groups allows individuals to challenge their stereotypes and discover that they are unfounded.

- **Deutsch & Collins (1951)** found that white Americans in racially mixed areas had more positive attitudes to black people than those in segregated areas.
- *But* de-segregation of schools in America increased prejudice, suggesting that simple contact is not sufficient.

social identity theory and prejudice reduction

Social identity theory (SIT) explains how prejudice can arise – through *social categorisation*, *identification* and *comparison*. These processes reinforce stereotypes that underpin prejudiced decision-making:

- Attention is drawn to differences between groups when they are categorised.
- The differences are stressed as individuals identify themselves as belonging to their group.

Finally, as groups are compared:

- in-group members discriminate, boosting their self-esteem by devaluing other groups.

SIT therefore offers three routes to reducing prejudice:

- minimising opportunities for categorisation by mixing members of different social groups together (*inter-group contact*);
- limiting identification by giving members of conflicting groups a shared purpose (*co-operation*) or building up the identity and status of the out-group (*collective action*);
- ensuring that members of other groups are valued (*co-operation* and *equal status contact*), i.e. making comparison less damaging.

political correctness

'Politically correct' language can alter social constructs, so referring to 'people with a disability' rather than 'the disabled' shifts the focus from *having a disability* to *being a person*. The use of 'gay' or 'black' as insults acts to maintain negative stereotypes so should be stopped.

collective action

The self-esteem of the out-group (often the minority) can be raised by political activism, such as feminism, which can lead to legislation to protect the rights of groups that are discriminated against. However, legal changes may not result in alteration of behaviour or attitudes.

making inter-group contact work

Aronson, Wilson & Akert (1994) suggested inter-group contact was more effective if groups:

- depended on each other;
- shared common goals;
- had equal status;
- could interact informally, on a one-to-one basis;
- had multiple and varied contacts between them;
- established a social norm of tolerance.

In a situation that met these criteria, **Bowen & Bourgeois (2001)** found that university students who shared rooms on a corridor with gay people were less homophobic.

co-operation

- Gaertner et al. (1989) argued that groups could develop a shared identity by working towards a common goal.
- This works in lab settings (Gaertner et al., 1990) and in real situations such as footballers from rival teams (Arsenal, Leeds, etc.) co-operating to play for England.
- But real-life groups may have conflicts that prevent them from co-operating.

social identity theory and the in-group favouritism

Groups of Internet users are able to make *social categorisations* and develop strong *social identities*, i.e. they find ways to determine whether other users are members of the in-group or not and to display their own group membership. They can then discriminate, boosting the value of their own group against others – *social comparison*.

Expertism is a way to categorise in- and out-group members, e.g. by laying a trap for the out-group (trolling) as illustrated by Wallace (1999).

However, even recent research about Internet social groups may already be out of date as the medium has become so widely available its users are so much more diverse.

the Internet and collective action

The Internet offers rapid, global communication so enables minority group members to keep in contact, strengthening *social identification*. Facer et al. (2003) describe Asian girls using the Internet to explore Islamic culture.

The Internet has been used to circulate information and assist in the organisation of protests to assist collective action in situations such as resistance to California's anti-immigration laws (Eng, 1995) and the Tiananmen Square pro-democracy demonstrations of 1989.

Internet interaction: is it an issue?

- The Internet is an increasing common forum for interaction, through email, chat rooms, interactive games and messaging.

- There are potential benefits to Internet links, such as for people with communication or mobility difficulties.

- The Internet may therefore be a medium for change in terms of discrimination and a platform for minorities to raise their profile.

- There are some potential hazards that people should be aware of, such as paedophiles taking on different identities.

what's different about Internet interaction?

- Immediate cues are missing. The facial expressions, tone of voice and posture of the communicator are absent.

- Most users rely solely on text, so they can omit or change information about themselves.

risk to children: yes or no?

- Children may indeed be at risk from people with assumed identities; Lamb (1998) found that two-thirds of people on 'children's' websites were, in fact, adults passing as children.

- However, evidence suggests that Internet interactions also benefit children directly as they, too, can alter their image or be accepted without prejudice based on their youth. Holloway & Valentine (2003) report children being able to interact with higher status people they admire (e.g. to get tips for their interests) and with people they like but wouldn't approach face-to-face for fear of being rebuffed or laughed at. Once contact was established, the children felt confident about real meetings.

the Internet and equal status contact

Almost all the information we make available about us on the Internet is by choice. Revealing age, gender or ethnic group is optional, but would be evident face-to-face. Wallace (1999) reports that, on the Internet, questions about race are rare. This means that many barriers are reduced or absent so interactions are much more equal, e.g. Keisler et al. (1984) found that, unlike face-to-face conversations, in emails the individual with the highest status did not necessarily dominate the interaction. Stigmatised individuals may therefore find the Internet a less threatening medium, e.g. Mickelson (1997) found that stressed parents of children with special needs preferred the Internet to other sources of support.

the Internet, equal status contact and reducing prejudice

Equal status contact is necessary for prejudice reduction (see page 9). The Internet facilitates this because status cannot be readily determined so grounds for *social categorisation* are reduced. Walther (1993) showed that people were less likely to make strong judgements about other group members after one Internet session but did after one face-to-face session.

However, the increasing use of webcams will erode the potential for anonymity.

research methods

The sales staff at Basketfull are multi-ethnic and a researcher from the local university is interested in the attitudes of Basketfull shoppers so they conduct a survey outside the shop.

- What is a survey?
- Describe **two** strengths and **two** weaknesses of this method.

contemporary issue

Caroline makes good friends with some of the girls at Basketfull and begins to talk to them about someone she 'met' over a year ago through a chat room on the Internet. He says he's 20, just two years older than her, and seems so nice and definitely keen on her too. She really liked him and wanted them to meet up, but when she suggested it he seemed to back down. She described to the other girls how she carried on writing even though he was being a bit strange. They suggested it might be dangerous to meet up – she might not know what she was getting into. Eventually, he mentioned going to a pub where she happened to have been the previous summer that was the popular choice for the local young people who were deaf – his reticence finally became clear – he, too, was hard of hearing.

- Use your understanding of theories from the social approach to discuss aspects of Internet interaction raised by this example. Refer to the situation described above in your answer.

theories

- Define the term 'obedience'.
- Outline **two** theories of obedience.
- Describe how **one** of these theories could account for the way Caroline obeys Simon's requests.
- Describe **two** strengths and **two** weaknesses of this theory.
- Outline **two** theories of prejudice
- Explain how **one** of these could account for the bullying behaviour of the group of girls.
- Assess this theory in terms of its strengths and weaknesses.

obedience and prejudice

Caroline has started a new weekend job at Basketfull, her local supermarket. On her first day Simon, one of the members of full-time staff at Basketfull, tells her to make tea and wash up. Since he is more experienced, she does as he asks. While she's at the sink, she listens to Simon entertaining the other Basketfull staff with funny stories. They seem to really like him, and when he suggests going out after work, they all want to go. The next day, Simon is really friendly to her; he seems to get on with everyone! He says that she should go outside to collect trolleys because the shop's image in the district is important. Caroline doesn't think it's her job, but does it anyway. While she's outside, she watches a group of girls in school uniform bullying another girl who seems to be from a different school as her uniform isn't the same as theirs.

studies

- Identify **one** study from the social approach.
- Identify the research method that it uses.
- Describe the findings and conclusion of this study.
- Explain how the study you have identified relates to the social approach. (*Hint:* Many studies in the social approach aim to test theories of obedience or prejudice, although there are many other ways that a study could relate to social psychology.)
- Outline **two** criticisms of the study you have identified.

application

The girls that Caroline saw came from two schools that have a history of ill-feeling between them. Describe and evaluate strategies that might be employed to reduce the prejudice exhibited between students from different institutions.

general assumptions

Two general assumptions from social psychology are the influence of individuals and culture.

- One individual can affect another, as in the case of obedience. Identify a study that illustrates this.
- Some individuals are very effective at getting others to obey them. Name a theory that accounts for this.
- Cultures differ in their use of language, for example, the meaning of 'gay' has changed from meaning happy, to homosexual, to a term of abuse. What theory can account for the changing understanding of language within a culture?

theories

- What is meant by the term 'prejudice'?
- Describe social identity theory.
- Describe **two** strengths and **two** weaknesses of this theory.
- Apply this theory to the situation described below.
- Describe **one** alternative theory of prejudice that could explain aspects of the situation described and illustrate how it would apply to this context.

contemporary issue

Men and women in the armed forces today are expected to sign to say that they are responsible for their own actions and efforts are made to encourage them to think critically about whether always to follow instructions.

One reason for this is to minimise the risk of repeating the horrors of the Second World War during which orders were followed without question and the consequence was genocide.

- Use your knowledge of social psychology to assess how effective these steps will be in guaranteeing to avoid blind obedience during wartime.

studies

- Identify **two** studies from the social approach.
- Describe the results and conclusion of both studies
- Explain how **one** of the studies you have identified relates to the social approach. (*Hint:* you could relate the findings to the situation described or to obedience.)
- Describe **two** strengths and **two** criticisms of **one** of the studies you have identified (and remember to indicate which one it is).

obedience and prejudice

Vince is a keen football supporter. He reckons that he can tell at a glance whether any other person on the bus he's travelling on to the match supports his team (Uptown United) or the opposition – Central City. Some of the ways he can tell are obvious – their scarves and shirts – but he believes there's more to it than that. He says all the Central City supporters are the same (and says a lot of other things about them that we won't put in print here). Compared to Uptown United fans, who he says are all dedicated, genuine and friendly, Central City fans are violent and devious. Vince says wearing his Uptown scarf makes him feel good – part of the 'extended team'. Despite his claims that Uptown fans are jolly nice sorts, they still hurl abuse at Central fans as they walk into the stadium.

general assumptions

Two general assumptions from social psychology are the influence of groups and society.

- In relation to the example of Vince, outline a way in which one group might influence another.
- Outline evidence that supports such influence of groups.
- Society can also exert an influence on individuals. Describe **one** way this might occur.

One way to see whether Central fans were more violent than Uptown fans would be to provoke each group by staging a fight and recording how quickly they joined in.

research methods

- Which research method is being used in the study described above?
- Identify and describe **one** ethical issue that the study would raise.
- Describe **two** advantages and **two** disadvantages of this research method.

application

Consider a situation of prejudice between 'boffins' and 'luddettes' (non-computer literate girls) in a school.

- Outline **two** strategies that could be used if prejudiced behaviour between groups of 'boffins' and 'luddettes' became problematic.
- Evaluate **one** of these strategies, discussing evidence for its strengths and weaknesses.

What stereotyped beliefs might this image reveal?

chapter 2
the cognitive approach

what you need to know   14

general assumptions   15

theories of memory   16

theories of forgetting   17

studies in detail   18

research methods   19

application   20

contemporary issue   21

questions   22

the cognitive approach

Cognitive psychology looks at mental processes such as perception, thinking, language and memory.

what's it about?

general assumptions

You need to understand and be able to describe at least **two** general assumptions of the cognitive approach:

- the use of the **computer analogy** for human cognition;
- the **information-processing** model of receiving, interpreting and responding to information.

theories

in-depth areas of study

You need to be able to describe and evaluate:

- **two** theories of memory, e.g.
  - **levels of processing** (Craik & Lockhart, 1972);
  - **multistore model** (Atkinson & Shiffrin, 1968);
- **two** theories of forgetting, e.g.
  - **cue dependence** (Tulving, 1972);
  - **motivated forgetting** (Freud, 1894).

You will also need to be able to apply these theories to situations for the key application and contemporary issue. For this, you may want to know a little about other theories such as displacement or decay.

classic research   research now

studies in detail

You need to be able to identify, describe and evaluate in detail **two** studies from the cognitive approach, e.g.

- **Craik & Tulving (1975)** – the levels of processing laboratory experiment looking at how different types of sentences used to encode words in different ways affect recall;
- **Aggleton & Waskett (1999)** – the 'smelly museum' field experiment of cue dependence that tested memory for displays at the Jorvik museum.

research methods

methods

You need to be able to outline and discuss research methods commonly used in the cognitive approach including:

- **experiments (laboratory);**
- **case studies of brain damaged patients.**

It is helpful if you can also:

- remember an example of each of these methods being used in cognitive psychology;
- identify the two kinds of experiment (laboratory or field, see pages 46 and 8).

real lives

key application

You need to be able to answer the question:

How accurate is eyewitness testimony?

To do this you should be able to discuss the link between theories in cognitive psychology – that is theories of memory and forgetting as well as ideas like reconstructive memory – and the research that supports them.

You need to be able to apply the theories to the problems facing eyewitnesses and police interviewers so that you can explain why eyewitnesses have difficulty remembering the events they have seen, what factors tend to make their recall more reliable, and how witness accuracy can be improved.

You should know some extra evidence (such as the Loftus studies) that relates directly to eyewitness testimony.

talking point

contemporary issue

You will need to use your knowledge of the cognitive approach to explain a current issue, such as **flashbulb memory**.
For this you will need to:

- be able to describe the issue;
- use **at least one concept** from the cognitive approach to explain the issue (e.g. one or more theory of memory and/or forgetting);
- use terminology from the cognitive approach.

You can also be asked to apply the concepts to a contemporary issue you have *not* studied.

the information processing model

what is the information processing approach?

- The information processing approach arose out of behaviourism, an approach that focused exclusively on observable behaviour – recording the direct and visible relationship between a stimulus and a response. The information processing approach developed because it is also important to consider what is happening between these two events.

- Between the receiving of a stimulus and making a response, the incoming information must be processed. This is the focus of the information processing approach.

- This processing might include perception (detecting information and making sense of it), memory (storing and retrieving information) or interpretation (understanding information).

- The approach describes the intervening events as a flow of information. This processing may be 'bottom-up', which means that the decision-making is based on the incoming stimuli, or it may be 'top-down', which means it is based on information already in the system which is used to interpret or understand the stimulus material.

why is the information processing approach useful in psychology?

- It provides a way to think of the structure (*hardware*) and functions (*software*) of the human mind.

- It allows us to investigate cognitive events which cannot be directly observed.

- Both the stimulus and the demands of the response can be systematically varied in experiments so it is possible to rigorously test the effects on processing, for example how quickly or accurately a task can be performed.

the computer analogy

what is the computer analogy?

- One way in which the flow of information can be described is by comparison with a computer.

- We can compare the input, storage and output mechanisms of humans and computers, as well as their processing capacities.

- Computers have keyboards, hard drives and audio outputs; we have senses, long-term memories and can talk (there are many other physical – hardware – similarities).

- Both computers and people have powerful processing abilities – although computers are better at algorithms (working things out systematically), whereas people are better at heuristics (guesswork)!

how does the computer analogy help in psychology?

- The similarities between human information processing systems and computers mean that we can use computers for models of human thinking.

- As computers become more sophisticated, e.g. being able to parallel process (do two things at once), they become an even better analogy for human information processing.

- This can be useful, e.g. in understanding where problems might lie when cognition deficits arise, such as in amnesia or loss of speech.

strengths of LoP

- Supporting evidence from well-controlled laboratory experiments, e.g. Craik & Tulving (1975), shows that more deeply processed information is better remembered.

- Physiological evidence (e.g. Nyberg, 2002) shows that semantic information results in more brain activity, which could equate to deeper processing.

- It has practical applications, e.g. viewers will remember adverts better if they process them semantically (Nordhielm, 1994), and students learn better if they semantically process (Riding & Rayner, 1998).

levels of processing theory (LoP)

- **Craik & Lockhart (1972)**
- Memory is a by-product of the processing of information.
- More deeply processed information is recalled better.
- Three levels of processing:
  - *structural* (what it looks like – shallow processing);
  - *phonemic* (what it sounds like – intermediate);
  - *semantic* (what it means – deep processing).
- LoP accounts for why some memories are recalled better than others – because the well remembered ones have been more deeply processed.

weaknesses of LoP

- The theory is incomplete as it cannot account for all variation in memory. Other factors, such as emotion (Reber et al., 1994), affect recall independently of depth of processing.

- The definition of *deep processing* is circular, 'depth' cannot be identified independently of its effect on recall.

- Conflicting evidence from studies such as Bransford et al. (1979) suggest that the apparent effects of deep processing might be better explained by something else, such as distinctiveness.

what is memory?

Memory is the store of information that has been encoded and retained and can be retrieved or accessed.

strengths of MSM

- Experiments (e.g. Glanzer & Cunitz, 1966) show that items at the beginning and end of a list are well remembered. This is because the early items (primacy effect) are rehearsed and passed from STM to LTM and stored there. The later items (recency effect) are recalled from STM. Items in the middle of the list are lost as they are displaced from STM before being rehearsed.

Probability of recall

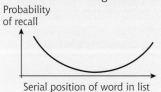

Serial position of word in list

- Studies of brain damaged patients (e.g. Scoville & Milner, 1957 – study of HM) show that STM can be lost independently of LTM so they must be different.

multistore model (MSM)

Atkinson & Shiffrin (1968) suggested that differences in recall arose because information was passed from one store to the next and they have different properties (of *encoding* – the form of representation used, *capacity* – how much information can be stored, and *duration* – the length of time that information is retained). If information is 'lost' at any stage, it cannot be recalled.

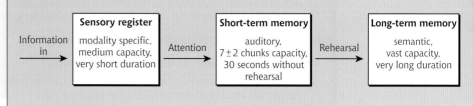

weaknesses of MSM

- Further evidence has shown that memory systems are more complex than MSM suggests, e.g. there are separate STM stores for different modality information because tasks involving sums and words do not necessarily interfere (Seitz & Schumann-Hengsteler, 2000).

- Information in STM, as well as LTM, can be semantically analysed (Forde & Humphreys, 2002 – study of FK).

- Evidence (e.g. Scoville & Milner, 1957 and Forde & Humphreys, 2002) suggests that LTM consists of several stores for different kinds of information (e.g. facts, events in your life, physical skills).

strengths of cue dependency

- Supporting evidence from well-controlled experiments (e.g. Godden & Baddeley [1975] – divers study [context]; Aggleton & Waskett [1999] – smelly museum study [state]) showed that presence of cues reduces forgetting. Duka et al. (2001) found that learning under the influence of alcohol produced better subsequent recall with alcohol (a state effect). Similarly, learning having drunk a placebo (believed to be alcohol but was not) resulted in better recall without alcohol.

- It has practical applications, e.g. for education. Abernethy (1940) found that students performed less well if they sat exams in a different room from their learning. Jerabek & Standing (1992) showed that context reinstatement during exams (by imaging the classroom) helped to improve recall.

cue dependency

- **Tulving (1972)** suggested that *cues* are extra pieces of information that help to locate an item in LTM and may be stored at the same time as the memory.

- *Context cues* are features of the environment that trigger the location of a memory (e.g. a smell, sight or place).

- *State cues* are internal triggers, which may be physiological, cognitive or emotional (e.g. a drug or mood).

- When appropriate cues are absent, state or context-dependent forgetting occurs.

forgetting: memory failure?

- Forgetting may occur because information is 'lost' during processing (availability failure), or because it cannot be successfully retrieved (accessibility failure).

- Alternatively, forgetting may occur because retrieval is actively denied, this would not be a memory 'failure'.

- Forgetting may occur in STM or LTM or may appear to arise when information was in fact never stored.

weaknesses of cue dependency

- Context and state effects may not be different. It may simply be that particular contexts evoke corresponding states, so all effects are, in fact, state-dependent.

- It is incomplete because some emotionally charged memories appear to be very well remembered (e.g. flashbulb memories) while others are forgotten (e.g. in repression).

strengths of repression

- Field experiments (e.g. Walker et al., 1997) show that unpleasant events are less likely to be recalled, suggesting that they are repressed.

- Diary studies (e.g. Myers & Brewin, 1994) have shown that defensive (but not anxious) participants are less able to recall unhappy memories suggesting that they have reduced anxiety by repressing unpleasant memories.

repression

- **Freud (1894)** suggested that traumatic memories are retained in our unconscious so we cannot consciously access them.

- This process of *repression* is a defence mechanism to protect us from negative emotions.

- Repression may act only on the emotions attached to an event so that we can recall what happened but not how we felt.

- A lesser form of repression is the general tendency to remember happy memories more readily than unhappy ones.

weaknesses of repression

- It is unethical to conduct laboratory studies as they would need to induce strong negative emotions. The existing evidence is less well controlled so effects may be due other factors, e.g. cue dependence.

- Much of the evidence for repression comes from case studies, which may be atypical, so the findings may not generalise to other individuals.

- Since repressed memories are unavailable, they are difficult to study. Therefore there is little evidence about how common they are or what causes them to occur.

- Some traumatic experiences (that should be repressed) cannot be forgotten.

strengths of Craik & Tulving

- It was a well-controlled experiment because there were equal numbers of questions in each of the category types.

- The validity of the measure of recall was improved by the surprise nature of the test – participants were not expecting to be tested so would not have made a special effort to memorise the words. This ensured that storage could only be a by-product of processing.

Craik & Tulving (1975)

Aim: to test whether processing words for meaning, sound or shape produced better recall as a way to find out whether deeper processing produces better recall.

Procedure: participants (who thought it was a test of reaction speed) had to respond 'yes' or 'no' to a list of questions. These caused target words to be processed structurally, phonemically or semantically (by asking questions about capital letters, rhyming or categories), e.g.

level of processing	example question	
structural	Is the word in capital letters?	PAPER
phonemic	Does the word rhyme with windy?	hedge
semantic	Is the word a kind of food?	melon

Later, the participants were given an unexpected test for the target words.

Findings:

level of processing	% recall of target words
structural	15
phonemic	35
semantic	70

Conclusion: deeper processing does result in better recall.

weaknesses of Craik & Tulving

- This was a laboratory study, testing people's memory for artificial lists. The laboratory may have been unfamiliar so participants could have paid more attention to their surroundings than to the task and in real life we are not generally required to answer these sorts of questions. These factors reduce the ecological validity of the study.

- Participants could have processed words with 'structural' questions in phonemic or semantic ways, reducing the validity of the test as a measure of LoP.

strengths of Aggleton & Waskett

- This was a field study, testing people's memory for real-life experiences (memory of the museum exhibits) so has good ecological validity.

- Order effects were accounted for by counterbalancing. Participants were questioned with smells presented either first, second or not at all. This controls for possible practice effects – any benefit to memory that might be gained by cues from the questions asked.

Aggleton & Waskett (1999): smelly museum study

Aim: to test whether distinctive smells present during encoding of information would affect recall of information, as a test of cue dependent memory.

Procedure: participants were volunteer visitors to a museum which featured characteristic smells. When re-contacted six or seven years after their visit, the participants completed a questionnaire about the museum twice. Sometimes this task was accompanied by bottled smells from the museum.

Findings: if the smells accompanied either the first or second questionnaire, they improved recall of the museum exhibits compared to absence of the smells.

Conclusion: the smells provided cues to assist recall of information about the exhibits.

weaknesses of Aggleton & Waskett

- The sample consisted only of members of the public who chose to visit the museum and who volunteered to take part in the study and were still willing and available by the second test opportunity. This sample may not be representative of the general population so the findings may have limited generalisability.

- Participants who chose not to participate after six or seven years may have been those who felt they could not remember very much. The results may therefore have been unreliable.

strengths of experiments

- Rigorous controls limit the effects of extraneous variables so that any changes in the DV are more likely to have been caused by the IV (increasing validity).
- Precise control of the experimental situation ensures that replication is possible (increasing reliability).
- Repeated measures designs limit the influence of participant variables because each individual acts as their own control, so any differences between conditions must be due to the IV.
- Independent measures designs reduce the impact of demand characteristics.

experiments

- Have an independent variable (IV) and a dependent variable (DV).
- Predict that the IV will have a causal effect on the DV.
- Look for cause and effect relationships.
- Use controls to limit the effect of variables other than the IV on the DV.
- Have two or more 'conditions' or 'levels' of the IV that are (in the case of laboratory experiments) manipulated by the experimenter.
- Use measures of the DV that ensure that the results are valid and reliable.
- Use different designs with the same, or different, participants doing each level of the IV.

weaknesses of experiments

- The contrived environment may be unlike real life in specific ways that matter to the participant or the situation, thus ecological validity may be low.
- Focusing on specific variables may lead researchers to overlook other, important factors affecting behaviour.
- Experiments tend to 'average' behaviour rather than looking for exceptions, so individual differences are ignored.
- Participants' behaviour may result from demand characteristics rather than the IV.

strengths of case studies

- Case studies enable researchers to investigate the effects of brain lesions in humans that it would not be ethical to study experimentally.
- They generate rich, detailed data.
- They provide a way to investigate atypical instances that may be rare thereby providing information that is unusual.
- It is possible to study factors that may be overlooked in experiments or other more rigorously controlled studies.
- Researchers can look at the way many factors may be involved in a complex situation because case studies use many different methods.
- Triangulation, which uses different techniques to research the same phenomenon, increases validity in case studies.

case studies of brain-damaged patients

- Case studies are detailed, descriptive investigations.
- They investigate a single instance, e.g. one person, family or organisation.
- Case studies may utilise other techniques, such as interviews or observations.
- Using cognitive tests, researchers can draw conclusions about the functions normally performed by the damaged brain areas.

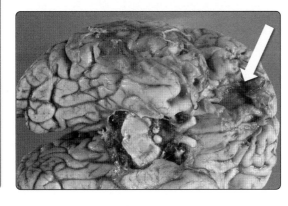

weaknesses of case studies

- The researcher may lack objectivity if they get to know the individual well.
- The researcher may be subjective and overlook a key aspect because of theoretical bias. This reduces validity.
- Results are unlikely to generalise to other people because it is unlikely that any two instances are identical.
- The extent of brain damage cannot be ascertained by a case study alone.
- The researcher cannot be certain that any behavioural or cognitive effects are due to brain damage as there are unlikely to be baseline measures of ability.

the multistore model

- In order for facts (such as details of faces or car registration numbers) to be encoded in memory, they must be attended to so that they enter the sensory store – if the witness isn't looking, they won't see (although they may later believe that they have).
- Information must be rehearsed in order to *transfer it from STM to LTM* – if events happen very quickly the earlier memories may be forgotten because of displacement.

the decay theory

- Information stored in STM *fades* or 'decays' within 30 seconds unless it is rehearsed – witnesses may not rehearse because events are unfolding very quickly so they are unable to or because they don't know that what they have seen is important.
- Memories may decay from LTM – so if it is a long time before they are asked to report what they have seen, it may have been forgotten. However, it is more likely that such memories are hard to retrieve rather than lost altogether.

cue-dependency

- Retrieval from LTM is affected by cues, such as *context* – an eyewitness recalling events at a police station or in court will not have the cues present in the environment of the crime to prompt their recall.
- Cues from the witnesses' *state* may not be available to increase access to memory – they may have been afraid or startled at the time of the event but not when reporting it later.

an eyewitnesses who sees a crime:

- is likely to have only a brief opportunity to memorise the scene;
- may not have been concentrating on the key events or individuals;
- is unlikely to be able to record what they have seen immediately;
- will experience a delay between the event and making a statement to the police or in court;
- will probably not return to the scene of the crime to report what they have witnessed;
- will not be in exactly the same state (e.g. of confusion) when they make their statement as they were as a witness;
- may have been very frightened during the event;
- may have their memory distorted by leading questions and other post-event information.

levels of processing

- The witness is unlikely to have the opportunity to deeply process information about actions, people or objects.
- Events may not appear to have any significance when they occur, so they are only processed at a shallow level.
- Events may happen so quickly that the witness has no time to consider the meaning so cannot process semantically.

repression

Unpleasant memories may be pushed into our unconscious by the defence mechanism of repression – if witnesses are traumatised by their exposure to the crime scene they may not be able to recall it.

leading questions

The witnesses' memory of the event may be distorted by post-event information. Discussing what they have seen with others, being questioned by police or cross-examined in court can influence the accuracy of their recall. Loftus conducted many experiments, which showed that:

- the wording of questions can distort memories, altering the accuracy of a witnesses' report of the scene, for instance their judgement of the speed at which a car was travelling;
- questioning can also supplement memories, causing witnesses to 'recall' aspects of the scene they did not see.

Cognitive interviews can improve recall by providing cues (linking to cue dependency) and avoiding leading questions. Witnesses (or victims) may return to the scene of the crime (providing actual context cues plus, possibly, state cues as a result). Context and state can also be reinstated by imagining or describing the event, thus providing new routes to access forgotten information.

multistore model

The long-term memory (LTM) component provides both very long term and detailed storage but this is limited and forgetting occurs. Flashbulb memories are claimed to be immune to these forgetting processes.

Because flashbulb memories relate to key historical events, they may be well remembered, not because the memories themselves are special but because the material is frequently rehearsed.

levels of processing

As flashbulb memories relate to events of historical importance, we may process the information at a semantic level, searching for meaning in them. This deep processing would result in good recall.

Neisser & Harsch (1992)

Questionnaires used to test Americans' recall of the Challenger space shuttle explosion found that, after four years, much of what was remembered differed from reports the same individuals had given the day after the disaster. The flashbulb memories seemed no more accurate than other long-term memories, even when participants were very confident about their accuracy.

However, there was neither a control group nor control questions to act as a baseline for non-flashbulb memories over the same time span and levels of affect (emotion), that are central to flashbulb memories, were not measured.

are flashbulb memories special?

According to Brown & Kulik (1977), flashbulb memories:

- are unusually vivid, accurate and long lasting;
- are caused by important events that are also shocking or surprising (i.e. linked to an affective response);
- may include trivial aspects of the environmental context in which they were encoded.

flashbulb memories

Can you remember where you were when you heard about the death of Princess Diana or the attack on the World Trade Centre in New York? You may have very vivid memories of these events, being able to recollect minute details of the situation you were in, or who you were with, in addition to being able to clearly recall the details of the event. Such 'flashbulb' memories are apparently especially accurate, lasting memories for specific moments in time ... *but are they?*

Bohannon (1988), Bohannon & Symons (1992)

Recall of both flashbulb and non-flashbulb memories for the Challenger disaster were tested at four times after the event. Consistency and detail of memory related to affect – people who were more 'upset' had more consistent and accurate recall. Memory for the non-flashbulb items, such as when it happened and what the weather was like, was also good.

However, the initial, baseline test of recall was conducted after two weeks had elapsed. The memory could already have changed by then. The control questions arguably also tested flashbulb memory as they were closely related to the event itself.

decay theory

This would suggest that flashbulb memories should fade over time like any other memories, but Brown & Kulik argue that having a special mechanism for emotionally shocking and personally relevant information would offer a selective advantage to those who could remember, enabling them to avoid the threat of potential disasters in the future.

cue dependency

Forgetting, according to this theory, occurs not because material is lost but because it is inaccessible. Aspects of the individuals' state or context at the time of encoding act as cues to subsequent recall. The cues for such tragic events are highly salient, so may act to retrieve both flashbulb memories and other information associated with the event.

Davidson & Glisky (2002)

They found that emotionally arousing memories (about the news of Princess Diana's death) were better retained by older adults with reduced frontal lobe function than memories of Mother Theresa's death. The flashbulb memories associated with the death of Princess Diana must have been qualitatively different from the less emotionally charged memories of Mother Theresa's death.

research methods

- What method could be used to study Janice's memory loss?
- Outline this research method.
- The nurses say that several other patients have similar problems whilst others seem to learn names easily. Jacob thinks it would be interesting to compare the number of nurses that each patient can name two weeks after coming onto the ward from intensive care and two months later. He suspects that some patients would show a clear improvement while others would not.
- Identify the method Jacob is proposing.
- Describe **two** advantages and **two** disadvantages of this method.

contemporary issue

Janice still can't remember John's name but they talk about where they were on 9/11. Most people on the ward can remember and Janice suggests to John that since the pattern applies to nearly everybody, including the nurses, it must be a special kind of memory. John's reply says both it is and it isn't special.

- Write an answer to Janice that justifies both viewpoints.

theories

- Outline **one** theory of memory that could account for one aspect of Jacob's memory for his grandmother's birthday.
- Explain how this theory accounts for Jacob's recall.
- Describe **two** advantages and **two** disadvantages of this theory.
- Identify **two** theories of forgetting that could account for why Jacob forgot about her birthday.
- Describe **one** of these theories in detail.
- Evaluate this theory in terms of **two** strengths and **two** weaknesses.

memory and forgetting

Jacob is a sixth-form Psychology student. He is on work placement in a local hospital with a ward for patients with head injuries and is on his way home when suddenly remembers it's his grandmother's birthday the next day. He wonders what made him remember. Perhaps it was because he caught a whiff of roast dinners – just like Gran cooks, or because his dad had spent all morning saying 'don't forget to visit your grandmother tomorrow'. As soon as he gets home, however, he forgets again. He had started thinking about one of the patients on the head injuries ward, Janice, who doesn't seem to be able remember the names of the staff even though she has been there for several weeks. She can, however, remember the names of all her friends and family who visit.

general assumptions

One general assumption from cognitive psychology is the information processing approach. This suggests that incoming information is encoded, processed, stored and retrieved for use, for example to control a behavioural response. One or more of these stages could be damaged in a patient with memory deficit.

- Identify one stage and suggest how a processing problem could affect their memory.

Another general assumption is the computer analogy. This suggests that each memory stage can be compared to a computer.

- Use this model to indicate how the stage of damage you identified above would affect a computer system.

studies

- Identify **two** studies from the cognitive approach.
- Describe the aims and procedures of both studies.
- Answer **either** part (i) **or** part (ii):
  (i) Assess how **one** of the studies you have described relates to the theories you have identified above and/or to Jacob.
  (ii) In what ways are the procedures of the two studies that you have described similar and in what ways are they different?

application

One patient was injured in a hit-and-run accident on a sunny day. Lots of witnesses came forward but they can't agree on the appearance of the driver or the car he was driving.

- What might Jacob say to explain why the witnesses may not be able to recall the incident clearly?

research methods

One way to test which of the ideas was the most effective would be to set up three trial sites using the different techniques and expose groups of participants to each of the screens for the same length of time.

- Name this research method.
- Outline the key features of this method as used in the cognitive approach.
- Explain **two** advantages and **two** disadvantages of this method.
- Suggest **one** alternative research method that could be used to test the effectiveness of the ideas.
- Outline this alternative method.

theories

- Describe **one** theory of memory that could account for why film C is likely to produce the best recall.
- How could this theory explain the differences in users' recall (C produced the best recall, A the poorest).
- Outline **two** advantages and **two** disadvantages of this theory.

studies

- Identify and describe **one** study from the cognitive approach.
- Evaluate this study in terms of **either** its strengths **or** its weaknesses.

contemporary issue

One contemporary problem for psychologists is the issue of patients' memory for the medical information that they are given. For example, patients tend to have poor recall for details of how to take medication they have received in short consultations with their GP. Similarly people who are very ill are often unable to remember what their consultant has said following their diagnosis.

- Use your understanding of cognitive psychology to explain why memory for medical information may be impaired and suggest ways that it might be improved.

general assumptions

- Which general assumption from cognitive psychology would be most relevant to explaining how details provided to patients about their medication (as described above) flows through the cognitive events of encoding, understanding, storage and retrieval? Describe this general assumption and outline how it applies to this situation.
- One way to think about the situation below left is to consider the roles of the senses, the brain and its instruction to the body in order to understand the resultant behaviour. Which general assumption would provide a model for these structures and events? Outline this general assumption and draw a table to illustrate how it applies to this situation.

memory and forgetting

A clothing company called Fittas is introducing a new winter clothing range and wants to add features to its website that will trigger people's memory so they return to the site more often. They run a competition to see what ideas the employees have, and the winners explain their proposals at a board meeting. The three selected are:

- **A: an animated visual of a man walking through the snow wearing a Fittas coat and scarf and a huge smile;**
- **B: a sequence of a man walking through the snow wearing a Fittas coat and scarf with 'Walking in a winter wonderland' as the background tune. A banner along the bottom of the screen reads** *Fight the freeze with furry Fittas!*
- **C: a film of a man zipping shut his suitcase in the boiling heat of summer, a brief shot of him on a plane looking out the window at snowy mountains then watching all the baggage except his arriving. He wanders along to the next carousel where there's a Fittas box going round and round. He grins, collects it and saunters off.**

application

Fittas has had several break-ins and is worried about losing stock. On each occasion, lots of local people were around at the time but they couldn't remember much about what they saw or heard. The residents themselves are concerned because the situation may lead to an increase in household burglaries. Fittas embarks on a joint venture with the local university and the police to plan ahead and arm the population with strategies to help them to provide better eyewitness statements if they do see anything suspicious.

- Use your understanding of cognitive psychology to make recommendations and justify your suggestions using evidence from psychological theories and studies.

chapter 3
the cognitive-developmental approach

what you need to know	26
general assumptions	27
Piaget	28
Vygotsky	30
research methods	32
application	33
contemporary issue	34
questions	35

the cognitive-developmental approach

Cognitive-developmental psychology looks at the advances in mental processes such as reasoning as children (and adults) change over time.

what's it about?

general assumptions

You need to understand and be able to describe at least **two** general assumptions of the cognitive-developmental approach:

- the **importance of cognitive abilities** – how they are essential for survival;
- the **development of cognitive abilities** over time – the effects of nature and nurture.

theories

in-depth areas of study

You need to be able to describe and evaluate **two** theories of cognitive development:

- **Piaget's** theories relating to:
  - **schemata and operations**;
  - **children's reasoning**;
  - **stages of development**;
- one other theory, e.g. **Vygotsky**.

You will also need to be able to apply these theories to situations for the key application and contemporary issue.

classic research / research now

studies in detail

You need to be able to identify, describe and evaluate in detail **two** studies from the cognitive-developmental approach, e.g.

- **Piaget & Inhelder (1956)** – the clinical interview of children looking at a three mountains model that tested for egocentricity;
- **Baillargeon & DeVos (1991)** – the experimental study that observed babies' reactions to the surprising non-appearance of a carrot.

research methods

methods

You need to be able to outline and discuss research methods commonly used in the cognitive-developmental approach including:

- **observation**;
- **longitudinal studies**.

It is helpful if you can also remember an example of each of these methods being used in cognitive-developmental psychology (Baillargeon & DeVos used observations in their experimental study and Bradmetz [1999] was a longitudinal study).

real lives

key application

You need to be able to understand and discuss links between cognitive-developmental theories and education.

To do this you should be able to use theories to give examples of, explain the reasoning behind and evaluate the effectiveness of some strategies, such as:

- discovery learning;
- child-centred learning;
- the readiness approach;
- scaffolding;
- the spiral curriculum;
- co-operative group work;
- peer tutoring.

talking point

contemporary issue

You will need to use your knowledge of the cognitive-developmental approach to explain a current issue, such as **the use of computers in education**.

For this you will need to:

- be able to describe the issue;
- use **at least one concept** from the cognitive-developmental approach to explain the issue (e.g. Piaget's and/or Vygotsky's ideas);
- use terminology from the cognitive-developmental approach.

You can also be asked to apply the concepts to a contemporary issue you have *not* studied.

the importance of cognition and cognitive abilities

how are cognitive abilities essential for survival?

Children need to:

- understand their physical and social world; e.g. being able to classify all things with big teeth as dangerous keeps a child from being bitten;

- be able to cope with change (since new, unfamiliar things could pose a threat). Processes called accommodation and assimilation allow even infants to adapt to new situations and predict future events using frameworks of understanding called schemata;

- learn how to reverse actions such as finding the way out of a building having found the way in, or getting down from a tree once they've climbed up. Schemata are too simple for this, but over time more sophisticated, operational thought appears that makes this possible;

- work things out, e.g. using formal reasoning in school with a view to earning a living;

- understand other people so that they can interact effectively, for instance by remembering faces, using language and interpreting the behaviour of others.

Why is cognition important?

- As these points illustrate, abilities such as memory, thinking and problem-solving are vital for living and are essential because they underlie language and socialisation.

- For example, being able to see the world from someone else's perspective – called decentration – would allow a child to work out when they might get hit in a fight.

the development of cognitive abilities over time

how do cognitive abilities change over time?

- Nature provides us with a limited range of responses at birth – reflexes – such as the startle response.

- Both nature (genetically controlled maturation) and nurture (environmental influences) affect the changes in children's abilities.

- Initially, children are motivated to learn through discovery, e.g. by exploring what they can do with or to their environment.

- Other external influences, such as models or people to assist them, can influence a child's understanding.

- However, at each age (or stage) children are able to understand progressively more sophisticated concepts.

- For example, very young children do not understand that physical things are permanent fixtures in the world, even when they cannot see them.

- Older children still have some problems such as being unable to see the world from the perspective of another person.

- Finally, children must acquire the ability to think in terms of symbols and concepts rather than actual physical objects.

Piaget: how children learn

The nature of children's thinking changes. They initially only use schemata, developing operational thought later – first concrete operations, then formal operations. They learn through active discovery.

- A *schema* is an internal model for understanding an aspect of the world.

- New ideas cause *disequilibrium*. In response, schemata are adapted by *assimilation* (the inclusion of new information) or *accommodation* (when information is too different so a new schema must be produced). This re-establishes *equilibrium*.

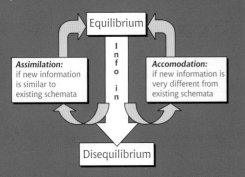

- Assimilation and accommodation together are the processes of *adaptation* – the way a child expands its understanding of the world using schemata.

- *Operations* are more complex rules for understanding logic and relationships between schemata.

- *Concrete operational thinking* is reliant upon 'real' objects or ideas.

- *Formal operational thinking* allows us to consider hypothetical ideas and real but unrepresented possibilities, i.e. it uses symbols in thought and abstract concepts.

evidence for changes in children's thinking

In addition to evidence from Piaget's own studies, many others have shown that young children do have specific problems with understanding (see below and right) showing that egocentrism, a lack of object permanence, failure to conserve and concrete thinking are typical characteristics of early cognitive development.

the pendulum test of formal reasoning

What matters?

- The push?
- The weight?
- String length?

Piaget & Inhelder (1956) gave children a pendulum and asked them to find out which factor affected the speed of the swing. Younger children randomly altered one or more factors, older children were systematic, varying only one variable at a time – they showed abstract reasoning. (NB It's string length!)

conservation experiments

Testing *conservation of number*: the child saw two even rows of counters and said they contained the same number.

If one row was then spread out, the child said there were more counters.

In a test of *conservation of liquid quantity*, the liquid was poured from a shorter, fatter beaker to a taller, thinner one. The children said there was more.

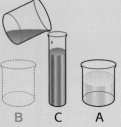

A   B

B   C   A

In both cases, younger children believe that the amount has changed when the appearance changes; they cannot conserve.

Piaget & Inhelder (1956): three mountains test of egocentrism

Using a model of three mountains and illustrations of the scene, children were asked to say which view a doll (placed opposite them) could see. Children under 7 years old found this difficult, tending to choose the view they themselves could see; they were egocentric.

Piaget: children's reasoning

- *Object permanence*: knowing it still exists even if you can't see it.
- *Egocentrism*: seeing the world only from your own point of view.
- *Animism*: attributing lifelike features to inanimate objects.
- *Conservation*: knowing that an object or quantity stays the same even if it looks different.

demonstrating object permanence

Piaget found that a child under 8 months will not look for a toy it has seen being hidden, even when its shape is visible under a sheet, because the child lacks object permanence. Older children search for the toy but, until they are 18 months, will stop looking if it is not where they saw it being 'hidden'.

Piaget

strengths of Piaget's stage theory

- Evidence shows that the cognitive abilities Piaget described do exist.

- Further research has also shown that children's thinking is different from that of adults and becomes more sophisticated, as Piaget proposed, e.g. Li et al. (1999) found that ability to conserve increases with age.

- Evidence supports the differences between stages proposed by Piaget, e.g. Wilberg (2002), for the preoperational/concrete operational distinction.

- It has provided useful guidance for education (see page 33).

did you eat the last biscuit? DID YOU EAT THE LAST BISCUIT? ...

Children expect that, when an adult asks the same question twice and something has changed they want a different answer. **Samuel & Bryant (1984)** tested this with number and liquid quantity conservation, comparing: standard Piagetian tasks, a task where the children didn't see the change and one in which they were only asked the post-change question. Both new designs produced a higher incidence of conservation but older children were still better than younger ones. So, Piaget's method made the task too hard for younger children to succeed.

Piaget: stages of development

Children pass through all the stages in the same order and they cannot skip one, i.e. the order is *invariant*. Each represents a new and more advanced level of cognition. The ages, however, are approximate.

stage	abilities	age (years)
sensorimotor	acquire object permanence	0–2
pre-operational	egocentric	2–7
concrete operational	learn to conserve, lose egocentricity	7–11
formal operational	acquire abstract thinking	11 +

findings on conservation: are they all the same?

McGarrigle & Donaldson (1974) repeated Piaget's conservation of number experiment but the counters were moved by a naughty teddy that ran across them in front of the child. They found that this 'accidental' transformation did not result in as many errors. Children as young as 4 years could answer correctly that there were the same number of counters in each row.

formal reasoning: when does it develop?

Bradmetz (1999) followed 7-year-olds for nine years and found less than 2% were capable of formal reasoning at age 16.

weaknesses of Piaget's stage theory

- Much evidence suggests children acquire abilities at different ages than Piaget suggested. Early changes were under-estimated, e.g. Hughes, Baillargeon & DeVos , McGarrigle & Donaldson, and later ones over-estimated, e.g. Bradmetz.

- Evidence, such as Vygotsky, suggests that Piaget attached too little importance to the role of people in children's learning. Although children are both curious and self-motivated, their cognitive development also benefits from interaction with others.

- The theory was based on studies that can be criticised on methodological grounds. Asking two questions in conservation tasks introduced demand characteristics and the three mountains task was unfamiliar.

egocentricity from another perspective

Hughes (1975) asked children to 'hide' a boy doll from one, then two policeman dolls in a model of cross-shaped walls. Children as young as 3½ years could position the doll correctly, showing that they could decentre.

another look for the onset of object permanence

Baillargeon & DeVos (1991) found that 3-month-old babies looked for longer, indicating surprise, at an 'impossible' situation where a long carrot disappeared behind a screen but didn't reappear (as it should have) through a window. The babies were therefore showing an understanding of object permanence.

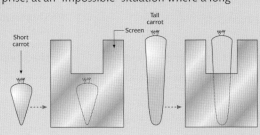

evidence for the ZPD

Wood (1991) describes how mothers can 'take down' their scaffolding when the child begins to learn on its own. A mother providing guidance for a 4-year-old building with wooden blocks may initially demonstrate, by assembling blocks. Later, she may just arrange them for the child, later only pointing to them, or giving direct verbal instructions such as 'get four big blocks'. Eventually the child will need only minimal scaffolding, with prompts such as 'now you make something'.

Vygotsky: how children learn

Vygotsky's ideas are similar to Piaget's in some respects:

- Children's thinking changes in characteristic ways as they develop.
- Their thinking becomes more sophisticated over time.
- Children need to interact with the world in order to progress.

But, there are also differences. Vygotsky believed that:

- language and social interaction were essential to development, especially for acquiring abstract thinking, whereas Piaget stressed exploration and the child's individual discovery;
- culture was important because thinking 'tools', higher mental functions such as problem-solving or art, could only be learned through guidance by other people so are embedded within a child's culture;
- people from different cultures would therefore have different cognitive 'tools' so different ways of thinking.

the zone of proximal development (ZPD)

ZPD
the potential level of understanding or ability the child could reach with assistance from others

the child's actual understanding or ability

ZPD: limits to children's learning

Social interaction with peers and adults can assist learning (and is essential to progress). Children can acquire some knowledge for themselves but are limited by their *zone of proximal development* (ZPD). This is the difference between the level of understanding a child can reach alone and the level it could potentially reach with help from others. This interaction may initially be direct instruction but can later be as little as someone asking a key question or giving a small prompt, i.e. the amount of instruction (called *scaffolding*) will reduce (see Wood, 1991). This progression is called the *learning cycle*.

are thinking tools culture-specific?

The idea of cultural differences in thinking is controversial as it could be used to imply that some cultures are better at thinking, although contemporary ideas suggest that different cultures have different (rather than better) 'toolkits' (Wertsch, 1991). For example, Salois (1999) found that, compared to American children, Native American children had poorer verbal ability but had better spatial ability.

does social interaction help learning?

Roazzi & Bryant (1998) asked 4- and 5-year-olds to work out how many sweets there were in a box on some weighing scales. Each child worked either alone or with another child who could help them but not tell them exactly what to do. Those with assistance received prompts that enabled most of them to succeed whereas those working alone didn't. Interaction with the other child helped the participants through their ZPD.

Vygotsky and the role of language

Piaget believed that language appeared when a child was sufficiently advanced and then progressed according to the child's stage of development. Vygotsky, in contrast, believed that language:

- appeared as a result of social interaction;
- initially serves only for communication;
- becomes crucial as a 'cultural tool' for further development.

This view explains why young children, in the pre-operational stage, think 'out loud' – they are learning to use language as a tool for thought. As they progress, this 'inner speech' becomes internalised and, by the concrete operational stage, it has become silent.

strengths of Vygotsky's theory

- There is good evidence that Vygotsky was right to criticise Piaget's under-estimation of the role of language and social interaction in cognitive development, as studies such as Roazzi & Bryant illustrate the value of interaction and instruction to learning.

- Evidence suggests that the nature of assistance given to children changes as they become more competent, supporting the idea of scaffolding through the ZPD (e.g. Wood). Similar patterns are seen in adults' use of language to help children, initially they use child-like words then, as the child's understanding increases, they use the correct words (Meadows, 1995).

- Many studies show that children learn more effectively when they can interact (e.g. Oley, 2002 – see page 33; Lou et al., 2001; Roazzi & Bryant, 1998).

- There is some evidence for the idea that cultures differ in their thinking 'toolkit', such as from Salois (1999). This supports the idea that thinking strategies are acquired socially rather than developing in isolation as each child 'discovers' the strategies for themselves.

- Vygotsky's ideas have provided useful guidance for improving instruction in schools, e.g. through peer tutoring (see page 34).

weaknesses of Vygotsky's theory

- The role of language is less clear than Vygotsky suggested. Pre-operational and concrete operational children do not seem to differ in the manner predicted by the internalisation of language as a tool for thinking (e.g. Prior & Welling, 2001).

- There is some evidence to suggest that social interaction is not universally essential, as some individuals in some situations learn more effectively alone (Lou et al., 2001).

- Vygotsky's idea that children's cognitive development should be more advanced in cultures which actively 'teach' thinking is now viewed as ethnocentric, that is, narrowly focused on the type of culture from which he came – in which formal school was the norm. This implies (inappropriately) that such cultures would produce more advanced thinkers.

does interaction always help learning?

Lou et al. (2001) conducted a meta-analysis (combined the results of many studies) to investigate the effect of interaction between individuals on learning. They found that whilst many individuals benefited, some did not. This suggests there may be individual differences that result in some, but not all, people gaining from interaction during learning.

is inner speech important to learning? *yes or no?*

Vygotsky's ideas suggest that pre-operational, but not concrete operational, children should benefit from being able to externalise their thinking.

Yes

Sonstroem (1966) explored ways to help children who had been unable to conserve substance – understanding that a Plasticine ball rolled into a sausage still has the same amount. They found that encouraging the children to use language to describe how the shape was changing (in addition to watching and performing the action) helped them to succeed on the task.

Initially, Sonstroem's children were non-conservers:

    'same'   'different'

After using action, vision and language to experience the transformation, they could conserve:

'It's getting longer and thinner'   'same'

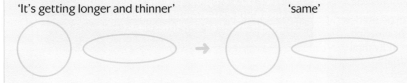

No

However, **Prior & Welling (2001)** tested children's comprehension of a passage they had read either silently or aloud. Surprisingly, there was no difference in the amount younger children had understood in each condition, but the older children's comprehension was better when they read aloud. This contradicts Vygotsky's idea that children initially use speech to help them to think and then internalise this speech.

strengths of observations

- Participant observation allows researchers to limit demand characteristics caused by awareness of being observed.
- A participant observer gains insight into the social context.
- A participant observer's records are more valid if they are integrated into the group by having the right characteristics such as clothing.
- Observations can generate either numerical or descriptive data providing either detail or the opportunity to use statistical testing.
- Reliability between two or more observers (inter-observer reliability) can be increased through training, e.g. watching and rating recorded behaviour together.

observations

- The researcher watches and makes detailed recordings of the participant's behaviour.
- Recordings may be done in different ways, such as by time sampling or event sampling.
- The observer may be part of the social setting (participant) or not (non-participant).
- A non-participant observer may be overt (obvious) or covert (hidden).
- Observations may be conducted in the natural environment (e.g. the home or familiar nursery school) or in a contrived one (e.g. a university laboratory) through one-way glass.
- The findings are analysed and interpreted.

weaknesses of observations

- Being a participant observer of a social situation may colour the observer's view so their records are subjective.
- To be effective, participant observation may require the participants to be deceived regarding the role of the observer.
- As a participant observer, it is difficult to record observations immediately, introducing errors into the data.
- If more than one observer is used, they may not obtain the same records from observing the same events, i.e. their inter-observer reliability may be low.

some general issues with studying child development

- Ethical issues arise as children may not be able to give fully informed consent to participate, although they should be asked in addition to obtaining consent from guardians.
- Researchers working with very young children may be unable to use some techniques that can be used with adults, such as interviews and questionnaires.

Zippo, zippa, zipper! Professor Ted's last moments of covert participant observation

strengths of longitudinal studies

- They do not rely on participants' memories for past events (unlike case studies) as data is recorded as events occur, so is more valid.
- Each individual can be used as their own control or baseline, so the influence of individual differences (participant variables) is reduced.
- They avoid cohort effects that occur when comparing people of different ages (because comparison across generations may find differences arising from culture rather than age).

longitudinal studies

- They trace changes in a group of individuals over a long period of time.
- The time period may vary from a few weeks to many years.
- They may employ a range of techniques including experiments, observations, questionnaires and interviews.

weaknesses of longitudinal studies

- Apparent improvements may be due to practice, relating to repetition of a test rather than an increase in cognitive ability.
- It takes a long time to collect results. Therefore they are expensive.
- Sample size declines with time as people leave the study because they lose interest, cannot be contacted or die.
- If a method or measure used at the start of the study turns out to be flawed, it cannot be changed as this would result in a loss of validity of the comparisons.

During the school years, children's cognition develops and they become capable of thinking in different ways. **Piaget's** ideas suggest that teaching should therefore be adapted to the needs of the child. This is the basis of *child-centred learning*. At each age, children will grasp new ideas most easily if they are presented in a way that suits their stage. So, with pre-operational children, teachers must be aware that they are egocentric and for concrete operational children, new material should be visual or even better, they should be able to actively 'discover' in a hands-on way. Later, during the formal operational stage, students can be given abstract tasks dealing with hypothetical situations as they are no longer reliant on concrete thinking. This is reflected in the expectations of the *National Curriculum*.

educational policy and practice

the influence of Piaget's and Vygotsky's theories

Vygotsky's ideas suggest that students should communicate with one another, discussing their work, as language is a means to think and learn. By using language to learn, children will acquire their 'cultural tools' more readily.

According to Piaget, each child works at a different rate. So within a classroom, children will have differing levels of understanding. Each child therefore needs to work independently, perhaps being seated at separate desks or having *individual learning plans* which determine the child's needs and targets.

Piaget's theory of cognitive development proposed that children develop in a sequential way through stages of development. During school age, these are *pre-operational, concrete operational* and *formal operational* thinking. The child's stage dictates what he or she can learn; children can only understand what they are ready for. At each stage, they must construct their own understanding through exploration. All children pass through the stages in the same order but at different rates.

Vygotsky suggested that children need to use language to develop their cognitive abilities and that this process equips children with the appropriate cultural tools for learning. Children also need knowledgeable people, such as more able peers or adults, to help them through the ZPD by *scaffolding* – providing enough information for them to continue to understand new ideas alone.

If children have reached the limit of their independent understanding, they will need prompts. This scaffolding is how teachers lead students through the ZPD. McCafferty (2002) showed that use of gestures by his teacher helped a foreign language student through his ZPD.

Although Piaget's ideas suggest that active learning should be better than passive 'chalk and talk', there is little evidence to support this.

Discovery learning is based on Piaget's idea that children need to explore for themselves, finding information to fit into their schemas and testing operations. Classrooms therefore need resources that children can use independently to work things out and build their own knowledge rather than just being 'told'.

The *readiness approach* requires that the teacher identifies when a child is approaching a stage transition, then gives them examples that relate to their new level of cognitive development to encourage their emerging abilities.

Children can gain *scaffolding* from *co-operative group work* in which students in groups help one another.

Peers can also help each other by offering scaffolding. This is called *peer tutoring*, in which a more able student scaffolds one who understands less about a topic. Foot et al. (1990) suggests that a child who has just understood a new concept is well placed to see the pitfalls for a peer who needs to be guided through their ZPD. Oley (2002) found that peer tutoring helped college students to gain higher grades on their essays.

Classroom evidence suggests that not all children benefit from group work (see page 34) which conflicts with Vygotsky's ideas and some may not work at all without teacher input.

According to Piaget, each child works at a different rate, so within a classroom children will have differing levels of understanding. This is easy to manage with computers as each child can work independently. Work can be planned to suit each child individually.

Computers can present information in different ways, e.g. visually or in abstract forms, to suit children at different stages of development. Papert (1980) suggested that this could help children to acquire formal operational thinking, so speeding up their development.

Piaget suggested discovery learning, which proposes that children should find out information for themselves to fit into their schemas or to test their operations. Computers are useful for assisting the process of discovery because the Internet, CD-ROMs, etc. have a large amount of very varied information to search.

Piaget's theory of cognitive development proposed that children develop in a sequential way through the same stages of development in the same order though at different rates and could only learn when they were ready. He also suggested that discovery learning was important as each child needed to explore for themselves.

However, the readiness approach also stems from Piaget's work, suggesting that teachers need to spot when each child is approaching a stage transition and present them with examples of problems that relate to their new level of cognitive development. It would be difficult for computers to make these assessments (without over-burdening the child with tests).

computers in education: good or bad?
the value of computer-assisted learning

Computers allow for students to communicate with one another (by email or chat rooms) which allows them to discuss ideas. This encourages the use of language as a means to think and learn as **Vygotsky** suggested, and so enables students to acquire 'cultural tools' for learning, not only the use of ICT but skills of interacting, searching, asking questions, synthesising information, etc.

Vygotsky suggested that children needed to use language to develop their cognitive abilities and that knowledgeable people, such as more able peers or adults, could help them through the ZPD by scaffolding.

It could be argued that the nature of communication using computers is different and perhaps less useful than face-to-face contact, especially as Vygotsky valued the cultural aspect of language and this may be lost in electronic interactions.

On-screen prompts can act as scaffolding to lead students through their ZPD. If the program is interactive, children can gain as much help as they need (Crook, 1994).

Peer tutoring using computers would allow more able students to scaffold ones who understand less about a topic. This would also apply if students were working in pairs with one work station. Mevarech et al. (1991) found that children who shared a computer for a task performed better on a later test than those who had a computer each, showing that co-operative peer tutoring with computers is beneficial. Lou et al. (2001) also showed that students working together on computers had higher achievement and satisfaction on average. However, some students did better alone, so working with computers in pairs doesn't suit all children.

Although on-screen scaffolding should improve learning, Bornas & Labres (2001) found that the achievement of children who used interactive software for maths was no better than those who did not. However, the thinking strategies used by the computer-assisted learning students were more advanced, suggesting that it might have helped with the acquisition of tools for learning.

theories

- Outline **one** theory of cognitive development that Dave could use to explain his changes.
- How would Dave have used this theory to justify his new ideas in the classroom?
- Describe **two** strengths and **two** weaknesses of this theory.
- Identify **one** other theory of cognitive development.

studies

- Identify **one** study from the cognitive-developmental approach that relates to **either** the theory you have described above **and/or** to Dave's situation.
- Describe this study in full.
- Explain how the study you have described relates to the theory you have described above and/or Dave's situation.
- Evaluate this study in terms of **two** strengths and **two** weaknesses.

research methods

- What method could be used to study how long each child spends concentrating on a task in Dave's classroom?
- Describe this research method in detail.
- Evaluate this method in terms of **two** strengths and **two** weaknesses.

children's changing cognitive abilities

A primary school teacher, Dave, takes up a new post in an old-fashioned school where all the desks are still in rows and the children work on their own. Dave decides to introduce some new ideas, starting with a project on History, which will mean that the children have to work in groups to plan how they will act out a battle. Initially he intends to help the children by offering them assistance with finding out how to investigate the strategies used and whether they can simulate opposing armies, but then allow them to explore and discuss the information between themselves and to develop their own plan for the re-enactment.

He expects to meet with some resistance because the headmistress, Miss Cluck, is adamant that children learn best when seated individually so that they aren't interrupted by other children and each can work at their own pace. However, other staff are very positive and his plan is implemented.

general assumptions

One general assumption from cognitive-developmental psychology is the development of cognitive abilities over time.

Nature provides us with a limited range of responses at birth – reflexes, such as the startle response. Both nature (genetically controlled maturation) and nurture (environmental influences) affect the changes in children's abilities. However, at each age (or stage) children are able to understand progressively more sophisticated concepts.

- Suggest **one** way in which an older and a younger child might differ in their understanding of either pain or language.

application

There are many ways in which the theory that you have described opposite can be applied to the classroom other than the changes suggested by Dave.

- Describe **two** other ideas, outlining how they relate to this theory and say how they could be put into action in a specific situation (e.g. teaching a particular subject).
- If you had to justify these ideas to Miss Cluck, what evidence would you use to defend your changes? Describe the evidence and explain how it backs up your decisions.
- What counter-evidence might Miss Cluck use to refute your argument? Outline one piece of research that she might refer to.

contemporary issue

- The most radical of Dave's ideas is to introduce a computer into the classroom. Write a letter to the parents of the children in his class that summarises the benefits of this idea.
- Produce a memo from Miss Cluck that offers a précis of the evidence against this idea.

theories

- Describe one theory from the cognitive-developmental approach that could explain why children of different ages have different educational needs regardless of their experience.
- Describe **two** strengths and **two** weaknesses of this theory.
- Outline the cognitive-developmental changes that:
  - (a) the 3-year-old has already experienced;
  - (b) the 4-year-old will pass through in the future.
- What are the potential benefits of the 'fun book' and the 'sand game' for each of the children in relation to their age and level of cognitive development?

application

Another mother at the playgroup is impressed with the ideas and asks Rachel and Fiona for advice on educational toys and games for her children, aged 1, 9 and 14.

- For any **two** of these ages, suggest a suitable choice (it can be a 'real' toy or a made-up one).
- Justify these choices in relation to one or more named theory(ies) of cognitive development.
- Use evidence from studies to explain why these choices are appropriate.

studies

- Identify **two** cognitive-developmental studies.
- State the research method used in each study.
- Describe the procedures of both studies.
- Explain **one** way in which the procedure of one of these is more effective than the other.

research methods

The 3-year-old attends a playgroup. Other mums at the playgroup have followed Fiona and Rachel's idea and several other, similar-aged children, have had 'fun book' input (although some have not).

- What method could be used to study differences in long-term development of children with early input from 'fun books'?
- Outline this research method.
- Describe **two** advantages and **two** disadvantages of this method.

children's changing cognitive abilities

Fiona and Rachel have a girl and a boy, of 3 and 4 years old respectively. They are employing lots of ideas to enhance their learning experience at home. For the 3-year-old, they produced a 'fun-book' with lots of big, colour pictures cut out from magazines on each page. They turn the pages, describe the objects, and compare them to things the child can see such as 'that's a canary, it's a bird like the robins in the garden'. One idea for their son is a set of shapes that can be filled up with sand. Each shape holds the same amount. The shapes can also be filled with Plasticine and the contents can be weighed on scales.

contemporary issue

Fiona and Rachel, like many parents, want their 4-year-old to have learned as much as he can before he starts school. They take him to a club in the local hall where there are lots of kids. They all have free access to a room full of equipment they don't have at home. Some older children from the area also attend to help the younger ones.

- Explain why their son might benefit from this opportunity.
- What potential educational disadvantages are there to this arrangement?

general assumptions

One general assumption from the cognitive-developmental approach is the importance of cognitive abilities. Cognitive abilities are essential for survival, for example, they enable us to use memory, thinking and solve problems so are vital for living. They are also important because they underlie language and socialisation.

- How well would an infant raised away from society as a 'wild child' cope if they did not have these cognitive abilities?

chapter 4
the learning approach

what you need to know   38

general assumptions   39

classical conditioning   40

operant conditioning   42

social learning theory   44

research methods   46

application   47

contemporary issue   48

questions   49

the learning approach

The learning approach looks at the mechanisms that are responsible for the ways we can acquire the potential to perform new behaviours.

what's it about ?

general assumptions

You need to understand and be able to describe at least **two** general assumptions of the learning approach:

- the **importance of the environment** – how the environment provides stimuli and consequences that affect behaviour;

- the **processes of learning** – e.g. the mechanisms that are common to a range of different learning theories.

theories

in-depth areas of study

You will need to be able to describe each of the following **three** explanations of learning. You will also need to be able to describe one example in humans, and evaluate the theory as an explanation for human learning:

- **classical conditioning**;
- **operant conditioning**;
- **social learning**.

Your examples of human behaviours may be the acquisition of:

- phobias (classical conditioning);
- language (operant conditioning);
- aggression (social learning).

classic research

research now

studies in detail

You need to be able to identify, describe and evaluate in detail **two** studies from the learning approach, e.g.

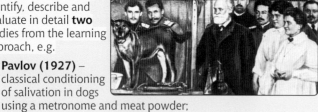

- **Pavlov (1927)** – classical conditioning of salivation in dogs using a metronome and meat powder;

- **Watson & Rayner (1920)** – classical conditioning of Little Albert to fear white objects like cotton wool after association of a frightening noise with a white rat;

- **Skinner (1948)** – operant conditioning of superstitious behaviour in pigeons through random reinforcement;

- **Bandura, Ross & Ross (1961)** – social learning of aggression in children after watching an adult behave aggressively towards a Bobo doll.

research methods

methods

You need to be able to outline and discuss research methods commonly used in the learning approach including:

- **laboratory experiments**;
- **animal learning studies**.

It is helpful if you can also remember an example of each of these methods being used in learning studies, e.g. Bandura (1961) was a laboratory experiment and Skinner (1948) was an animal learning study.

real lives

key application

You need to be able to understand and discuss links between learning theory and the deliberate alteration of human behaviour, e.g. in behaviour therapy.

To do this you should be able to use concepts and research from the learning approach to explain how behavioural therapies operate to alter human behaviour and the effectiveness of such strategies.

talking point

contemporary issue

You will need to use your knowledge of the learning approach to explain a current issue, such as **media violence**.

For this you will need to:

- be able to describe the issue;

- use **at least one concept** from the learning approach to explain the issue (e.g. conditioning or social learning theory);

- use terminology from the learning approach.

You can also be asked to apply the concepts to a contemporary issue you have *not* studied.

the importance of the environment

The environment affects behaviour.

- *It provides stimuli that are important in classical conditioning* as triggers for reflexes, such as the presence of meat in front of a dog that makes it salivate. In non-experimental situations, stimuli are important because they can trigger adaptive responses that have been acquired – we leap onto the verge of a country road because we have previously been scared by a close encounter with a vehicle on a bend.

- *It is important in operant conditioning* as it can provide cues for the performance of learned responses. For example, a rat can learn to make a particular action when the environmental stimulus of a light appears. Similarly, children learn to stick chewing gum under the desk when they see their teacher walking towards them (a stimulus from the environment) because they have been punished for chewing in class.

- *It provides consequences that shape behaviour.* For example, consequences such as food pellets or electric shocks can increase or decrease the frequency of a rat's behaviour. Likewise a child's behaviour, such as how often they clean their shoes, can be affected by reinforcement, e.g. praise, or punishment, (e.g. being told off).

- *It provides models that are important in social learning* as they can be imitated, allowing individuals to learn by observation. A child growing up in an environment where adult models have a regional accent will acquire that accent by imitation.

- *It provides sources of vicarious reinforcement that may be important in social learning.* For example, if a child observes a sibling being praised for finishing their meal, they are more likely to imitate the behaviour they have seen.

Although other approaches suggest that aspects of the external environment may affect behaviour (such as the psychodynamic approach which says childhood experiences are important or the physiological approach which says light and dark help to control daily rhythms), the learning approach is different because it focuses directly on the role of the environment. (Other approaches include internal aspects too, such as the unconscious in psychodynamic psychology or genes in physiological psychology.)

the processes of learning

Some learning mechanisms apply to a range of different theories. These common processes include:

- *generalisation* – producing a behaviour learned to one stimulus in response to other, similar stimuli, e.g. imitating aggressive behaviours seen performed with one toy, like a doll, but with another toy, like a teddy bear;

- *discrimination* – distinguishing between two similar stimuli and responding to only one of them, e.g. a zoo animal that has learned that food is delivered by keepers in blue uniforms will ignore the keeper if they wear different coloured clothes;

- *extinction* – the disappearance of a response when the learning situation is removed, e.g. if rewards are not forthcoming;

- *spontaneous recovery* – the reappearance of a learned response after extinction has occurred. For example, if a zoo animal has learned that keepers wear blue and then their uniform changes, the animals will, after a while, stop responding to blue-clothed people (extinction). However, they may later resume responding to blue clothes (spontaneous recovery).

These ideas are central to the approach because they apply to learned behaviours irrespective of the way in which they were acquired. They are also important because they have value for the learner. Being able to generalise a response means that it can be applied to additional situations which might be beneficial (e.g. birds that learn to open milk bottle tops can generalise this to yoghurt pots, cream tubs, etc. and gain new sources of food). Discrimination may allow an individual to avoid dangerous or unpleasant situations, for example learning to eat safe but not dangerous berries. Extinction in the absence of rewards avoids wasting effort, but 'trying again later' – spontaneous recovery – might be useful, for example, a bird should stop flying to an empty bird feeder, but returning to it a week later might reap rewards if it has been refilled.

classical conditioning: the mechanisms

Classical conditioning can only result in an individual learning to reproduce a behaviour they can already perform, but in response to a new situation. The learned response becomes an automatic and unavoidable consequence of exposure to this new stimulus. In order to describe this process, you need to understand the correct terms:

- *unconditioned stimulus* (UCS) – the existing cause of a behaviour prior to conditioning;
- *neutral stimulus* (NS) – a new stimulus that, prior to conditioning, does not produce a response;
- *unconditioned response* (UCR) – the existing response to the unconditioned stimulus;
- *conditioned response* (CR) – a response, similar to the unconditioned response, but produced in response to the CS;
- *conditioned stimulus* (CS) – the name for the neutral stimulus after conditioning, once it has acquired the capacity to produce the conditioned response.

The CR may differ from the UCR in terms of latency and strength; the response is likely to occur sooner and more strongly to the UCS than to the CS.

Pavlov (1927): Pavlov's dogs

Aim: to investigate why his experimental dogs salivated in response to the sound of footsteps, suggesting they had learned that the sound was associated with food.

Procedure: salivation was measured during:

- the presentation of meat powder alone;
- the presentation of meat powder and the ticking of a metronome (the conditioning phase);
- the ticking of a metronome alone.

Findings: the dogs initially salivated to the meat powder but not the metronome. After the conditioning phase, the dogs also salivated to the metronome.

Conclusion: the dogs acquired an association between the existing response of salivation and the new stimulus – the sound of the metronome.

prior to conditioning:
UCS (meat powder) → UCR (salivation)

during conditioning:
UCS + NS (beat of metronome) → UCR

after conditioning:
CS (beat of metronome) → CR (salivation)

Watson & Rayner (1920): Little Albert

Aim: to discover whether fear could be classically conditioned.

Procedure: the single participant was a 9-month-old boy who was unafraid of various objects, including a white rat, but was startled by a loud noise. He was conditioned by being shown the rat and simultaneously hearing a loud noise. This was repeated several times. His response to the noise alone was observed, and to objects (such as wooden blocks) that had not been associated with the noise. This was checked immediately after conditioning and seven weeks later.

Findings: the infant displayed fear to the noise (from a steel bar) and after the second pairing leaned away from the rat. After five days, he cried in response to the rat and similar white, soft objects (e.g. fur coat and Father Christmas beard). These responses were still present after seven weeks. He did not show distress in response to the wooden blocks.

Conclusion: the infant had acquired an association between the sight of the rat and the new stimulus – the loud noise – through classical conditioning. This response generalised to other, similar, white fluffy objects but not to different objects such as the wooden blocks.

prior to conditioning:
UCS (loud noise) → UCR (fear)

during conditioning:
UCS + NS (white rat) → UCR

after conditioning:
CS (white rat) → CR (fear)

strengths of Watson & Rayner

- Provides support for classical conditioning as an explanation of learning as Little Albert developed an association between the stimulus of the rat and the response of fear to the noise.
- Good controls: taking a baseline measure of fear to the rat and to the blocks meant they could be sure that his later response was due to the conditioning.

weaknesses of Watson & Rayner

- Because this was a single-participant experiment and Albert may have differed from other people, e.g. in terms of fear of or on exposure to fluffy things, the results may not be representative of the population or generalisable.
- The procedure was designed to make Albert afraid and, although this was discussed with his mother, it would contravene current ethical guidelines.

phobias: an example of classical conditioning in humans

Some phobias may be learned through classical conditioning and it can also provide a way to overcome such fears. The idea of *preparedness* suggests that we are more likely to become conditioned to objects that would have presented a threat during our evolutionary history, such as snakes which might be poisonous. If early humans were going to gain from such learning, they would have to acquire a fear very quickly. *One trial learning* is where an association is built up between a UCS and CS from a single pairing.

Ohman et al. (1976) tested the idea of preparedness by attempting to condition student volunteers to fear pictures of snakes, spiders, houses, flowers and faces:

brief, painful electric shock (UCS) → fear (UCR)

UCS + picture (NS) → fear (UCR)

picture (CS) → fear (CR)

For the prepared stimuli only (the pictures of snakes and spiders), the CS of fear (measured as an increase in galvanic skin response – sweatiness) was acquired in a single pairing (one trial learning). It was also more resistant to extinction than the fear learned to the non-prepared stimuli.

Systematic desensitisation is a technique based on classical conditioning that can be used to overcome phobias. The therapist:

- agrees an *anxiety hierarchy* with the client – a graduated sequence of feared stimuli (e.g. pictures, video, then live spiders that are increasingly big and hairy);
- induces a state of relaxation (UCR), e.g. using hypnosis or progressive muscle relaxation (UCS). Reciprocal inhibition prevents us from experiencing opposite emotions at the same time so fear is prevented by maintaining relaxation;
- pairs relaxation with the least frightening item on the hierarchy (CS);
- works up through the hierarchy maintaining relaxation in the client.

At the top of the hierarchy, the client will be able to stay relaxed when confronted with the feared stimulus itself (such as a big, hairy, living spider).

Zinbarg et al. (1992) found that systematic desensitisation was more effective than other treatments for phobias and Emmelkamp (1994) reported that it was effective for a range of phobias and other disorders such as PTSD.

strengths of classical conditioning as an explanation of human learning

- It can account for the acquisition of some human behaviours, such as food preferences. We may develop a dislike for foods that we happen to eat when we are sick (e.g. foods eaten by cancer patients receiving chemotherapy which makes them vomit).

- Evidence such as Ohman et al. (1976) shows how some responses are more readily acquired by classical conditioning than others. This illustrates the important role played by classical conditioning in survival – being able to learn rapidly that snakes or spiders are dangerous would have been valuable in our evolution.

- There is evidence for the effectiveness of behaviour therapies, e.g. systematic desensitisation and aversion therapy that are based on classical conditioning (see also page 47). These applications are used to help people overcome fears and addictions and so improve lives.

- In general, there is plenty of evidence for classical conditioning both in animals and humans so the results are reliable.

weaknesses of classical conditioning as an explanation of human learning

- It can only account for the acquisition of responses that involve the production of an existing behaviour in a new situation. It cannot therefore explain how we develop entirely new responses or complex ones. Since much human behaviour is complex, this is an important weakness.

- It is insufficient as an explanation as there are other ways in which humans learn, including operant conditioning, social learning and insight – a way of acquiring new behaviours with no overt conditioning phase. For example we could alternatively acquire a phobia by observing phobic behaviour in a parent.

- Systematic desensitisation can only be used with people who can maintain the imagery necessary for relaxation and who can transfer their learning from the safe environment with the therapist to their life outside.

- Systematic desensitisation only solves the problem of the consequences of the phobia not the cause, so is less effective than other forms of therapy that tackle the root of the problem.

exam note

You can also use the material described here on systematic desensitisation in the application for the learning approach (see page 47).

operant conditioning: the mechanisms

An animal responds to stimuli in its environment with a range of behaviours, some of which produce pleasant, others unpleasant, consequences. Such consequences dictate the future frequency of the behaviours that precede them. A behaviour that:

- has good effects (results in *positive reinforcement*) is repeated more often;
- causes bad effects to stop (results in *negative reinforcement*) is repeated more often;

- has bad effects (results in *punishment*) is repeated less often. The effect can be either the end of something nice (*negative punishment*) or the start of something nasty (*positive punishment*).

The consequences of a behaviour may occur every time the action is performed or only sometimes (*partial reinforcement*); this pattern is called the *schedule of reinforcement* and affects both the rate of responses and how quickly the animal ceases to respond in the absence of reinforcement (*extinction*).

schedule	frequency of reinforcement	response rate	extinction	example
continuous reinforcement	every time the behaviour is performed	low, steady it is reinforced	rapid extinction	pat the dog every time it sits
fixed ratio	every Nth performance is reinforced	high rate, post-reinforcement pause (prp) follows response	extinction quite rapid	get paid for every 50 newspapers delivered
variable ratio	occurrence of reinforcement is varied, averaging out at every Nth act	fastest rate, steady	most resistant to extinction	unpredictable rewards of gambling
fixed interval	reinforcement given at the end of every time period X in which the act has occurred	rate lower than ratio schedules, with prp	moderately resistant	getting pocket money at the weekend if your room is tidy
variable interval	occurrence of reinforcement is varied, averaging out at every time interval X in which the act has occurred	high, steady	gradual extinction	child writes tidily all day waiting for the teacher to look at their work and say well done

Skinner (1948): superstitious pigeons

Aim: to show that operant conditioning can create apparently superstitious behaviour in pigeons.

Procedure: eight hungry pigeons were tested in Skinner boxes for a few minutes each day. During this time they received a food pellet every 15 seconds regardless of their behaviour.

Findings: 75% of the pigeons developed repetitive behaviours, such as turning and hopping, that were not present before the experiment.

Conclusion: intermittent, uncontrollable reinforcement caused the pigeons to behave as though they believed that the arrival of food depended on their behaviour, i.e. to produce superstitious behaviours. Random consequences can increase the frequency of the behaviour they happen to follow – even when the reinforcement is not actually dependent on performance.

the Skinner Box

Skinner produced a mechanised way to present stimuli and administer rewards or punishment. The 'Skinner Box' allowed researchers to alter reinforcement schedules and record the frequency of behaviour. Rats, pigeons and other animals could be tested in a highly controlled environment.

Skinner used:

- stimuli (**A**ntecedents) such as lights;
- to trigger responses (**B**ehaviours), e.g. bar pressing, disc pecking or escape;
- that were then reinforced or punished (with **C**onsequences such as food or electric shocks).

Think **A → B → C**

An animal in a Skinner box explores, performing a range of behaviours, some of which will result in specific consequences (such as food pellets). A pigeon which receives a food pellet every time it happens to peck a disc will learn to peck the disc more often, a rat which can switch off an electric current by pressing a bar will rapidly learn to push the bar in response to the current switching on.

strengths of Skinner

- The behaviour of the pigeons was observed prior to conditioning so that it was certain that the subsequent behaviours were the result of learning.
- The environment was highly controlled, for example the automatic dispensing of food, so that other variables cannot have been responsible for changes in the pigeons' behaviour.

weaknesses of Skinner

- Superstitious behaviours were not acquired by 25% of the pigeons. This may have been because it was a small sample or because superstitious behaviour is not characteristic of all individuals.
- Although the food pellets were dispensed randomly, the pigeons may not have found them immediately, altering the timing of reinforcement.

language acquisition: an example of operant conditioning in humans

According to Skinner (1957), children acquire language through operant conditioning. Initially babies make noises – called babbling – and these are positively reinforced by people around them. This increases the likelihood that the infant will babble. Reinforcement will be more likely to occur if the noises sound like words, so the infant is selectively rewarded for speech-like sounds, and these will be repeated more often. Sounds that are not appropriate to the language are ignored by other people so are not reinforced. As a result, they are not repeated. This process of selectively reinforcing closer approximations to appropriate sounds (called *shaping*) continues so eventually the child produces actual words. These are reinforced not only by attention but because they result in the achievement of a goal – a child who can say 'bicci' is more likely to get the food it wants than one who just points; this is another source of positive reinforcement.

The effects of shaping continue to mould language learning. Accents and use of language such as swearing or jargon may be reinforced or punished by the approval, disapproval or understanding of others. For example, a child may swear because he or she enjoys the respect of friends or the annoyance it creates in adults.

strengths of operant conditioning as an explanation of human behaviour

- Operant conditioning can account for acquired differences in language, e.g. why English speakers lose the ability to produce certain sounds (such as the 'll' in Welsh) because they have not been reinforced for making this sound as infants.

- Applications of operant conditioning theory can help in guiding teachers and parents to reward children, thus improving their learning or behaviour.

- Operant conditioning shows why reinforcement is more effective than punishment – because rewards indicate the desired behaviour whereas punishment only informs us about what not to do.

- Effective therapies, e.g. token economies (see page 47) are based on operant conditioning which suggests that some of the problem behaviours they aim to reduce may have been acquired by operant conditioning in the beginning.

weaknesses of operant conditioning as an explanation of human behaviour

- Some aspects of language learning cannot be accounted for by operant conditioning or can be better explained by other theories. For example, children make persistent mistakes in their speech for which they cannot have been reinforced, e.g. saying 'I runned back home past the sheeps after I buyed my sweets'. These suggest that they are using rules (such as adding 'ed' or 's' to the end of words) rather than simply being shaped.

- Even when these errors are corrected, children continue to make them for a while suggesting that they are biologically pre-programmed for language as well as there being an environmental component to language learning.

- Studies on operant conditioning are based on generalisations, so may overlook individual differences.

- Operant conditioning cannot account for complex behaviours. Humans also use insight and reasoning.

- Much of the research on operant conditioning was done on animals which, since animals are simpler than humans, may not be valid.

- As an explanation, operant conditioning ignores other factors that could affect changes in behaviour, such as genetics.

exam note

Skinner did many studies on operant conditioning with rats and pigeons. If you are asked to 'describe a study' in an exam, you must make sure that it is one particular study, not a jumble of methods and findings from a number of different investigations.

The same also applies to studies conducted by Pavlov and Bandura – there are many similar ones so beware!

social learning theory

Social learning theory (SLT) says that social or observational learning is the process of acquiring the ability to perform a new behaviour by watching that behaviour in another individual (the *model*). The observed behaviour is then *imitated*. Behaviours acquired in this way can therefore be learned without necessarily being performed.

Bandura (1977) suggests four processes are required for social learning:

- *attention* – observing;
- *retention* – remembering;
- *reproduction* – being able to do the behaviour;
- *motivation* – a reason to perform the action.

All of these are necessary for the behaviours acquired through social learning to be demonstrated. Several other factors increase the likelihood of performing a behaviour acquired through social learning; if the:

- observer has seen the model being rewarded for the behaviour (this is called *vicarious reinforcement*);
- model is the same sex;
- model is powerful;
- model is friendly.

strengths of Bandura et al.

- The laboratory experiment was well controlled because the children were rated for aggressiveness to ensure that differences between groups were the result of the model's behaviour. There was a control group that saw no model to be sure that any effect was not just due to the presence of an adult, and both boys and girls saw male and female models.

- The children were frustrated to ensure that they all had a similar level of aggressiveness so that differences were due to the effect of learning, not how aggressive the observation had made them feel.

- The controls raised the reliability of the study and meant that it could be easily replicated.

- The findings have implications for real life as they show that children can learn aggressive behaviours from models such as characters on TV and their parents, so they could be used to guide TV scheduling and advise parenthood classes.

Bandura, Ross & Ross (1961): a Bobo doll study

Aim: to investigate whether children can acquire aggressive behaviour by observing models and whether the model's gender is important.

Procedure: 36 boys and 36 girls aged 3–6 years saw adult models playing. Initially each child was rated for aggressive behaviour and the groups were matched. Different groups saw:

- aggressive or non-aggressive behaviour by the model, or no model;
- same or different sex models.

The non-aggressive model played for 10 minutes with Tinker toys. The aggressive model played with the Tinker toys for 1 minute, then for 9 minutes displayed both verbal and physical aggression towards a Bobo doll. The children were then frustrated by being shown attractive toys which they could initially play with but were then told were for other children. Finally, the children were moved to another room with toys including a Bobo doll and observed for 20 minutes through a one-way mirror.

Findings: children, especially boys, who saw aggressive models showed more violent behaviour towards the Bobo doll than those who had observed non-aggressive behaviour. Girls reproduced slightly more verbal aggression and boys more physical aggression. Boys were more likely to imitate same sex models; the same pattern existed for girls although it was less evident. Children who saw the non-aggressive model were even less aggressive than those who saw no model.

Conclusion: observation and imitation can account for the acquisition of specific aggressive behaviours. Children are more likely to learn from gender-specific models.

weaknesses of Bandura et al.

- The sample was narrow because the age range was small (and older children are probably exposed to even more aggressive models) and all the children came from one nursery school (at Stanford University) so may have all been similar in important ways (e.g. the nursery may have had a particular policy on aggressive behaviour) so the results might not generalise to other children.

- The study raises ethical issues as the children's exposure to aggression detrimentally affected their behaviour. Ethical guidelines say that participants should not be negatively affected by research.

- The experimental setting was unusual as children are not normally deliberately shown aggressive acts, so they may have thought they were meant to copy them.

imitation of TV violence: an example of social learning in humans

The example of Bandura et al. (1961) shows that children will imitate aggression from a live model, but further studies by Bandura and others have shown that they will also imitate aggressive behaviour seen on screen.

Bandura et al. (1963) – *beware! see exam note on page 43* – compared the behaviour of children exposed to different aggressive modelling situations. They either saw:

- real-life aggressive models with a Bobo doll;
- the same models performing exactly the same behaviours but recorded on a colour film that was projected onto a screen 2 metres away;
- a film of an aggressive cartoon character 'Herman the Cat' presented on a TV. The film was made to appear as a cartoon and was acted by one of the models dressed as a cat who performed the same sequence of behaviours as in the other conditions;
- no film or live model (control group).

As in Bandura et al. (1961), the children were then frustrated and subsequently observed for aggression. The findings showed that all of the model groups displayed significantly more aggression (average score of 91) than the control group (average score of 54) although the differences between the effects of different models were small. In many of the categories, such as total aggression, imitative aggression, gun play and partially imitative aggression (such as sitting on the Bobo doll and using the mallet), the greatest effect was for the filmed model, suggesting that violent humans on film are potent models for aggression.

strengths of social learning as an explanation of human behaviour

- There are many studies that support the influence of different types of model on aggressive behaviour suggesting that this is an important aspect of human learning. Many are well-controlled laboratory studies and their similar results suggest the findings are reliable.
- Social learning includes both environmental factors such as models, the effects of reinforcement (in common with operant conditioning), cognitive aspects (e.g. retaining the information and the relative importance of different kinds of models) and motivation. It is therefore a more complete explanation of learning than other theories.
- Humans can appear to have acquired new behaviours without any learning; social learning can explain such situations.
- Social learning can help psychologists to understand the acquisition of behaviours such as aggression through exposure to violent television. This can be used to guide broadcasting restrictions.

weaknesses of social learning as an explanation of human behaviour

- Many factors other than social learning can affect aggression, e.g. operant conditioning (feeling powerful and 'winning' are positive reinforcers) and physiological factors (there may be genetic causes for aggression).
- Laboratory studies of aggression may be very artificial which can reduce the validity of the findings. For example, children may not hit a Bobo doll because they are imitating an adult's aggression but because they think that they have been invited to, because the situation is unfamiliar.
- Because behaviours acquired through imitation may not be demonstrated immediately, it is difficult to measure learning accurately. As a consequence conclusions based on studies of human social learning may be flawed.
- Social learning cannot account for the acquisition of entirely novel human behaviours that have not been observed in a model, so it is an incomplete explanation.

exam note

As this example shows, you can often make use of the same studies or ideas for more than one part of the course. The material discussed here is also used in the contemporary issue (see page 48).

strengths of laboratory experiments

- Rigorous controls limit the effects of extraneous variables so that any changes in the DV are more likely to have been caused by the IV, thus increasing validity.
- Precise control of the experimental situation ensures that replication is possible and tends to increase reliability.
- Repeated measures designs limit the influence of participant variables.
- Independent measures designs reduce the impact of demand characteristics.

laboratory experiments

- Look for cause and effect relationships.
- Have an independent variable (IV) and a dependent variable (DV).
- Predict that the IV will have a causal effect on the DV.
- Are conducted in contrived settings such as laboratories.
- Are readily controlled to limit the effect of variables other than the IV on the DV.
- Have two or more 'conditions' or 'levels' of the IV that are manipulated by the experimenter.
- Use different designs with the same, or different participants doing each level of the IV.

weaknesses of laboratory experiments

- The contrived environment is generally different from the participants' everyday situation because it is unusual and controlled in particular ways (that are different for each experiment). Also, it is focused on a single variable (the IV) which is also unlike real life so ecological validity may be low.
- Focusing on specific variables may lead researchers to overlook other important factors affecting behaviour.
- Experiments tend to 'average' behaviour rather than looking for exceptions so individual differences are ignored.
- Participants' behaviour may result from demand characteristics rather than the IV.

strengths of animal learning studies

- They can be more highly controlled than would be ethical or practical in studies of human participants.
- Replication is easy as many animals can be tested because they are small to house and cheap to keep.
- Animals can be used in procedures such as food deprivation that would be unethical or unpopular if attempted with human participants.
- Animals that are similar to humans, such as other mammals, particularly primates, are good models for human behaviour.
- Because an animal's environment can be controlled from birth, the researcher can be more certain that the appearance of a new behaviour is due to learning.

animal learning studies

- Are investigations of the mechanisms by which animals acquire new responses.
- Can test different learning theories.
- Use a range of species, e.g. pigeons and rats.
- Can be conducted in laboratory or naturalistic environments.
- Use apparatus such as the Skinner box and mazes.

weaknesses of animal learning studies

- Procedures such as food deprivation may cause animal suffering.
- If animals are distressed by the procedures of the study, this may affect the validity of the results gained from them.
- Findings from studies on animals may not generalise to humans because of differences in biology, learning capacity or the processes of learning.
- Animals may respond to aspects of the learning situation other than those intended by the researcher.

classical conditioning and behaviour change: behaviour therapy

Techniques that use classical conditioning to alter behaviour are called *behaviour therapies*. They work by controlling conditioned and unconditioned stimuli. Techniques include:

- *systematic desensitisation* (see page 41);
- *aversion therapy*.

behaviour change: how can an understanding of learning theories be used to deliberately alter human behaviour?

Learning theories rely on the effects the environment can have on behaviour. It is therefore possible, by changing aspects such as the pairing of stimuli or the timing of rewards, to deliberately alter people's behaviour. Techniques based on these principles are used in clinical settings to help people.

operant conditioning and behaviour change: behaviour modification

Techniques that use operant conditioning to alter behaviour are called *behaviour modification*. They work by controlling antecedents and consequences. One technique, used with school children, prisoners and some patients with mental illnesses, is called the *token economy*.

aversion therapy

Maladaptive behaviours such as alcoholism or smoking can be controlled by aversion therapy. This works by pairing an unpleasant CS with the behaviour to be eliminated. For example, a drug called Antabuse is used with alcoholics:

UCS (Antabuse) → UCR (vomiting)

UCS + NS (alcohol) → UCR (vomiting)

CS → CR (unpleasant expectation of vomiting)

The expectation of the unpleasant effects is aversive – it acts as a deterrent so the alcoholic avoids drinking alcohol.

token economy

The behaviour of individuals in schools, prisons and mental health institutions can be changed using operant conditioning. The performance of behaviours desired by the institution are positively reinforced with tokens – these may be coin-like objects, symbols such as merit marks or punches on an individual's card. The tokens can be saved up and exchanged for goods, e.g. CDs in schools, or privileges, such as watching TV in prisons. The tokens act as secondary reinforcers – they have no value themselves, but represent primary reinforcers. Secondary reinforcers acquire their reinforcing properties through classical conditioning, i.e. by association. The use of tokens provides a way to instantly reinforce individuals for appropriate behaviour so that it is repeated. The system can be used, for example, to encourage self-care behaviours such as washing and dressing in patients or to improve children's classroom or playground behaviour.

strengths of behaviour therapy

- Evidence suggests that aversion therapy is effective for a range of problems, e.g. Duker & Seys (2000) used it to reduce self-injury in children.
- Aversion therapy is more effective if an alternative behaviour is reinforced.
- See also page 41.

strengths of behaviour modification

- Tokens can be given immediately, so are effective reinforcers for the desired behaviour.
- Rewards are a more ethical way to modify behaviour than some other techniques.
- Evidence suggests that token economies are cheap and easy to administer and effective in a range of situations, e.g. with schizophrenic patients (Ayllon & Azrin, 1968).

weaknesses of behaviour therapy

- Generalisation in aversion therapy for alcoholics can cause them to dislike drinking any fluids at all.
- Aversion therapy has been used inappropriately, e.g. to 'cure' homosexual tendencies.
- Aversion therapy does not solve any underlying problem. For example, it can be used to limit compulsive eating but this does not deal with the cause (such as frustration) so is not a long term solution.
- See also page 41.

weaknesses of behaviour modification

- Token economies can only alter the performance of behaviours so do not solve the cause of the behavioural problem.
- Rewarding behaviours that should be performed without reinforcement (such as personal hygiene) may make transition out of the institution difficult.
- Ethical issues may arise as institutions have the power to deprive individuals of privileges that others may see as rights.

social learning theory

Through SLT, a behaviour can be learned without being performed, by *observing* and *imitating* a model.

Bandura (1977) suggests four processes are required for social learning:

- *attention* – watching;
- *retention* – remembering;
- *reproduction* – being able to do the behaviour;
- *motivation* – a reason to perform the action.

Media such as video and television provide such models, and children's behaviour is affected by what they see.

violence in the media: is it an issue?

The media, including TV, video, computer games and newspapers, have all been accused of being responsible for rising rates of violent behaviour. Is it possible that children are learning to be aggressive from violent media?

- Children are certainly exposed to media violence – Eron (1995) estimates that a child leaving primary school will have seen 8000 murders and 100 000 other violent acts on TV and video.

- Children as young as 2 years old can be influenced by what they see on TV. Troseth (2003) showed that children who had been filmed hiding a toy and 'watched themselves on TV' were more likely to be able to find the toy later.

evidence for the effect of media violence

- Eron et al. (1972) found a positive correlation between violence level of TV programmes seen by 8-year-olds and their aggressiveness.

- Eron & Huesmann (1986) followed this up and found that the more violent TV the boys watched as children, the more likely they were to be violent criminals as adults.

- Joy et al. (1986) studied Canadian children before and after the introduction of TV to towns and found a significantly greater increase in the incidence of aggression in those who had not already been exposed to TV.

do people copy what they see?

Bandura et al. (1961) showed that children would imitate the violent behaviour of a model towards an inanimate Bobo doll. Girls were more likely to reproduce verbal aggression and boys were more physically aggressive, each gender imitating the language or actions of the model (see pages 44 and 45).

the St Helena experiment

A natural experiment (Charlton et al., 2000) found that children on St Helena island, who had not previously seen transmitted TV, did not become more violent after satellite TV became available. Children aged 3–8 were observed in the playground before and after this change and, even though the violent content of programmes was a little greater than British TV, levels of violent behaviour remained the same. However, the children were initially exceptionally well behaved, so they may not have been a representative sample.

factors affecting imitation

Observers are more likely to imitate models that are:

- same-sex – *gender* ;
- high status – *status*;
- powerful – *power*;
- similar age – *age*;
- likeable – *personality*.

These effects occur because observers identify with models who they look up to, increasing imitation. Many TV heroes and heroines are likeable, important and powerful, so are effective models.

can observation affect the perception of violence?

Vidal-Vazquez & Clemente-Diaz (2000) found that simply showing violent films to adolescents increased their acceptance of, and attraction to, violent behaviour suggesting that TV violence may make aggression more acceptable.

how convincing is this evidence?

- Studies such as Eron's are correlational so a third factor, e.g. parental control, could be responsible for both the TV viewing and violent behaviour.

- Eron's initial data was from several decades ago and not all the subjects were followed up so the findings may not be generalisable.

- Not all studies find a strong link between TV viewing and aggressiveness, e.g. Milavsky et al. (1982) found family environment to be more important and Hagell & Newbury (1994) found young offenders watched no more violent TV than a control group.

theories

- What is meant by the concept of 'learning'?
- Describe the mechanisms of social learning theory.
- Apply this theory to the situation described in the central box.
- What is the term used to describe the process of rewarding those students who were performing the activity first?
- Explain how the praise for one student will affect the behaviour of the other student in the pair.
- Describe **two** strengths and **two** weaknesses of the social learning theory as an explanation for human behaviour.
- Compare and contrast this theory to any other theory of learning.
- Explain what is meant by the principles of *discrimination* and *generalisation* in the context of learning.

studies

- Identify **one** study from the learning approach.
- Identify the research method that it uses.
- Evaluate the study you have identified in terms of **two** strengths and **two** weaknesses.

contemporary issue

Miss Melcher has observed a decline in playground behaviour. Several children have been seen swinging their bags at each other's legs. She believes this is related to an advertisement for fruit juice that the children have seen on TV in which the 'Orange Man' pulverises little 'orange people' by spinning them around in a net of oranges to make fresh juice.

- Use your knowledge of the studies and theories from the learning approach to explain how such a pattern of behaviour could arise and whether evidence supports this explanation.

social learning theory

A teacher, Miss Melcher, is aware that some of her students are much better than others at joined up writing. In the next class she rearranges the seating plan so that each student who is having difficulty is sitting next to one who is doing well. She has organised them so that the student who is better at writing is always on the left. She asks each pair of students to demonstrate joined up writing to each other, starting with the student on the left. The classroom has an aisle half way back. For the pairs behind the aisle, Miss Melcher actively praises the student who is demonstrating the activity first. She spends as much time with the pairs towards the front but doesn't actively praise them.

Miss Melcher has decided to see how well her students learn with different kinds of rewards. They each do a task on a computer in the learning resource centre. In one version of the task every correct answer is rewarded with a flashing gold star that appears on the screen; in the other the student hears a round of applause for a correct answer.

general assumptions

One general assumption from the learning approach is the importance of the environment.

- In relation to the example described in the box, outline a way in which the children's environment could affect their behaviour.
- Outline evidence that supports such influence of the environment.

research methods

- Which research method is being used in the study described above left?
- Identify **one** study from the learning approach that uses this research method.
- Identify and describe **one** ethical issue that the study would raise.
- Describe **two** advantages and **two** disadvantages of this research method.

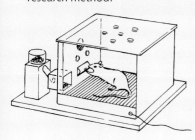

- What apparatus is this?
- Outline **two** strengths and **one** weakness of using this apparatus.

application

Following the escalation of violence, Miss Melcher decides that she will try to change the children's playground behaviour.

- Outline **two** strategies that could be used to change the children's behaviour.
- Evaluate **one** of these strategies, discussing evidence for its strengths and weaknesses.

theories

- Outline **two** theories of conditioning.

- Describe how **one** of these theories could account for Kylie's response to the music when she is at home.

- Identify **one** of these theories and describe **two** of its strengths and **two** of its weaknesses.

- Explain what is meant by the general principles of *extinction* and *spontaneous recovery*.

- Damian hates cats. Advice from a charity for protecting birds says to scare cats out of the garden by spraying them with water, which they don't like. How could Damian use a theory of learning to explain how this might work?

- He also wants to use a device that makes a high pitched noise that annoys cats. It generates the sound continuously and so they run until they are out of range and can't hear it anymore. Use a learning theory to explain how this works.

contemporary issue

Damian spends ages on the Internet and Kevin is worried because it seems to be an addiction. He emails the psychologist on a national newspaper to ask whether this could be a problem.

- Use learning theory to write a reply to Kevin presenting evidence that suggests people could become addicted to Internet use.

research methods

Kevin has an older son, Damian, who is studying Psychology at university. He is home for the holidays and decides to try to replicate, with Sharon's school gerbils, some work on rats he has read about. He makes a set of tunnels out of toilet roll middles stuck together with tape. They form a maze through which the gerbils can run to find food. In the paper that Damian had read, rats were either fed every time they reached the goal box, every other time, or unpredictably.

- Damian is conducting an animal learning study. Outline this research method.

- Describe **two** strengths and **two** weaknesses of this method.

conditioning

Kevin has two daughters. He discovers that Kylie, the youngest, falls asleep in the car because of the rocking motion. Whenever he has Kylie in the car and she's tired, Kevin puts the same track on the CD player. As a consequence, she always falls asleep to the same music. At home, when Kylie's in her cot, Kevin plays the same track and she falls asleep really quickly.

Sharon, Kevin's older daughter, has just started school and gets a merit sticker every time she has a tidy desk and peg at the end of the day. The children can save up their stickers to get a book voucher at the end of term. By Christmas, Sharon has enough stickers to get a book voucher for Harry Potter.

The children are also allowed to exchange their stickers for the chance to take the school gerbils home for the holidays. Sharon decides to do this instead.

studies

- Identify **two** studies from the learning approach.

- Describe the procedure, findings and conclusion of **one** of these studies.

- Outline **two** criticisms of the study you have described.

- Explain how the study you have identified relates to the learning approach.

  Hints:

  - Does it test a particular explanation of learning? If so, which?

  - Does it relate to either of the general assumptions of the learning approach?

  - Does it test an application of learning theory?

application

Jim, Damian's friend, is really scared of the cats. Damian says he needs therapy to help him to overcome this fear. Describe one or more therapies that might be used and explain how **one** of these would be applied to Jim's fear. How effective is this treatment likely to be?

general assumptions

One general assumption from the learning approach is 'the processes of learning'.

- Describe **two** of these processes.

- Outline how **one** of these processes could apply to the situation described in the central box.

chapter 5
the psychodynamic approach

what you need to know	52
general assumptions	53
Freud	54
Erikson	59
research methods	60
application	61
contemporary issue	62
questions	63

the psychodynamic approach

The psychodynamic approach considers the way unconscious motives affect our emotions and actions by looking at the past (our childhood events) and the present (symptoms of mental disorders, personality characteristics and symbolism such as in dreams or speech errors).

'Sometimes a cigar is just a cigar.'
Freud didn't say that everything in dreams was symbolic!

what's it about?

general assumptions

You need to understand and be able to describe at least **two** general assumptions of the psychodynamic approach:

● the **importance of the unconscious mind and motivation** – we are unaware of much of our mental processing but it can still affect how we feel and what we do;

● the **importance of early experience** – our behaviour and feelings in adulthood are affected by our childhood experiences.

theories

in-depth areas of study

You need to be able to describe and evaluate **two** psychodynamic explanations:

● Freud's theories;
● one other theory, e.g. **Erikson**.

For Freud, you will need to describe and evaluate the:

● **model of personality**;
● **defence mechanisms**;
● **psychosexual stages of development**;
● **dream theory**.

You will also need to be able to apply these theories to situations for the key application and contemporary issue.

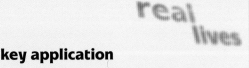

classic research / research now

studies in detail

You need to be able to identify, describe and evaluate in detail **two** studies from the psychodynamic approach, e.g.

● **Freud (1905)** – a case study, Little Hans, whose phobia of horses arose from an Oedipal conflict;

● **Adams et al. (1996)** – an experimental study of homophobia to demonstrate reaction formation as a defence mechanism.

research methods

methods

You need to be able to outline and discuss research methods commonly used in the psychodynamic approach including:

● **case studies**;
● **clinical interviews**;
● **analysis of symbols**.

It is helpful if you can also remember an example of each of these methods being used in psychodynamic studies, e.g. Freud (1905) – Little Hans – was a case study *and* used analysis of symbols. Brown & Harris (1978) used interviews.

real lives

key application

You need to be able to understand and discuss links between psychodynamic concepts and mental health, e.g. linking childhood trauma and adult mental disorder.

To do this, you should be able to use concepts, theories and studies from psychodynamic psychology to explain how early trauma can cause later mental health problems.

talking point

contemporary issue

You will need to use your knowledge of the psychodynamic approach to explain a current issue, e.g. **why we watch Buffy**.

For this you will need to:

● be able to describe the issue;

● use **at least one concept** from the psychodynamic approach to explain the issue;

● use terminology from the psychodynamic approach.

You can also be asked to apply the concepts to a contemporary issue you have *not* studied.

the importance of the unconscious mind and motivation

the unconscious mind and motivation

- There are memories and mental processes in our minds of which we are unaware. These are in our unconscious.
- It contains material that is hidden away so that we cannot access it, such as sexual and aggressive instincts.
- This can happen to memories from childhood or adulthood.
- One part of the mind (the Superego) has the role of hiding (repressing) unacceptable ideas from other parts of the mind (such as the Id).
- This process of hiding or disguising memories is achieved through the use of defence mechanisms.

This is important because:

- even though we cannot access these thoughts, they can still affect our behaviour, cognitions and emotions. For example, unconscious wishes or desires can motivate our actions;
- being unable to access hidden information helps to protect us from frightening, embarrassing or painful thoughts, such as fears, sexual desires and murderous intentions;
- memories from childhood that are hidden can affect us in adulthood through the content of our dreams or our mental health. For example, recall of episodes with an abusive parent may be repressed so that they cannot be upsetting but can cause other symptoms such as depression;
- this approach offers an understanding of aspects of our psychology that cannot be explained through any processes that require awareness.

the importance of early experience

childhood experiences

- For psychodynamic psychologists, any early experience may be significant but especially those relating to our parents and other important people in our lives.
- Psychodynamic psychologists also focus on experiences which present a trauma or conflict, such as ones causing sadness or fear.

This is important because:

- later behaviour and feelings are affected by childhood experiences;
- childhood experiences can also mould our adulthood personalities, e.g. trauma at different ages influences adult personality in different ways;
- mental health in adulthood may be related to successful or unsuccessful early experiences, e.g. loss of the mother during childhood may be linked to adult depression so the psychodynamic approach can offer ways to understand adult problems;
- if we can understand how adult mental health problems have arisen during early childhood, we may be able to resolve them;
- knowing about the role of early relationships is valuable because it has implications for child care.

defence mechanisms

Some thoughts can upset us, so these are made 'unavailable' by defence mechanisms – a kind of 'access denied' for your memories.

repressed memories

The unconscious mind contains thoughts, such as fears and memories, that are held there by **defence mechanisms**, such as repression. These thoughts may stem from **early childhood**, hence why it influences later life.

Id, Ego, Superego

Our personality has three interacting aspects – think of them as 'sides' or 'faces' of yourself. One part, the Id, is unconscious; the others are partly conscious.

- The Superego – the aspect that responds to authority – develops during childhood and the phallic stage is especially important.

- The Ego is responsible for 'censoring' memories by using defence mechanisms. It can also manage conflict between the Id and the Ego by using defence mechanisms.

unravelling the Freud maze

Freud's ideas can seem confusing, partly because they are abstract and the focus on sexual motives is hard to believe, but mainly because the research covers several different, interconnected concepts that you need to both distinguish, and see the relationships between. This page should help you sort out this problem: refer back to it after you have read pages 55–8.

the unconscious

Freud believed that part of our mind is unconscious. It can affect us even though we might not know what is in there (although other parts of our minds are accessible – the conscious and preconscious).

analysis of symbols

There are occasions when unconscious motives (e.g. from hidden desires or fears) cause changes in feelings or behaviour that indicate the existence of those repressed thoughts. Freud believed that, even though these events might be disguised, they could be interpreted – providing information about the individual's unconscious.

Dreams and slips of the tongue are examples, as the underlying motive is hidden so the symbolic representations (the dream or the spoken words) must be analysed to access the unconscious.

psychosexual development

Children pass through stages, initially driven by the Id, but by the phallic stage, the influence of childhood experiences will have had an important effect on the development of the Superego.

Events, especially traumatic ones, can affect the progress of development and so can account for differences in adult personality.

These effects show how important early childhood is to development.

mental health

Symptoms of mental illness, such as anxiety or depression, can be accounted for in two related ways, by the effects of:

- traumatic experiences during childhood;
- repressed memories on the development of the adult personality.

dreams

According to Freud, when we dream, unconscious thoughts are sometimes translated into different events in the dream story. So dream interpretation uses the symbols in dreams to explore the hidden meanings in the unconscious.

clinical interviews and case studies

Freud based his ideas on his findings from the symptoms, behaviours, speech and dreams of patients in therapy. His techniques allowed him to interpret this detailed information and come to conclusions about their unconscious.

psychosexual development in boys and girls

Oedipus complex (boys)
Awareness of penis → attaches to love object of mother → competes with (stronger) father for her affection → wishes him dead but fears him (suffers castration anxiety as notices girls have no penis) → represses love for mother and identifies with father.

Electra complex (girls)
Notices she has no penis (suffers penis envy) → attaches to love object of father (with a penis) → blames the mother for castration so fears her → substitutes desire for penis for desire for baby → represses love for father and identifies with mother.

Freud: topographical and structural models

Freud: levels of consciousness

the topographical model

Freud distinguished between three levels of consciousness:

- *conscious mind* – thoughts, perceptions and memories of which we are fully aware;
- *preconscious mind* – memories that we can become aware of under certain circumstances;
- *unconscious mind* – motives and memories that cannot be brought into consciousness, e.g. *Libido*, the life instinct that manifests itself as sexual motives, and *Thanatos*, the death instinct that manifests itself in aggression.

These three levels can be illustrated as a floating iceberg with consciousness above the water:

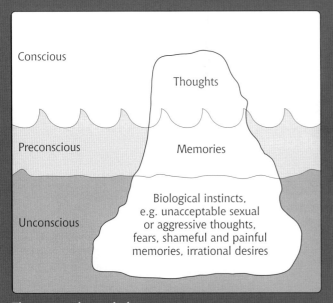

The unconscious mind:

- has no logic;
- can hold contradictory thoughts without conflict, e.g. loving and hating at the same time;
- makes no distinction between reality and fantasy;
- can use one object as a symbol for another;
- influences behaviour in ways that seem illogical, e.g. slips of the tongue, dreams or inexplicable impulses.

This model is useful because it helps to explain irrational behaviour, but it is difficult to measure or test objectively precisely because the unconscious cannot be accessed.

weaknesses of the structural model

- Concepts such as the Id and the Ego and, to an extent, instincts are very difficult to study objectively although this does not necessarily mean they do not exist.
- Much of the evidence for Freud's ideas comes from case studies which are subjective and difficult to replicate.

Freud: structural model of personality

Freud believed the personality was complex because there were three different aspects to the mind.
These three aspects can operate separately explaining why we feel inner conflict such as 'I'd really like to do it but I feel I shouldn't'.

name	aspect of personality	operating principle	role	example
Id *(it)*	instinct	pleasure principle	to ensure our biological needs, e.g. food, warmth, sex, are satisfied	I want to eat all those sweets
Ego *(I)*	logic	reality principle	balances the demands of the Id and the restraint of the Superego	I will eat one more, then stop
Superego *(above I)*	society's rules	morality principle	restrictions learned from parents, etc. that curb the desires of the Id	You shouldn't eat any more. It's bad for you.

strengths of the structural model

- Freud provided evidence for the influence of unconscious urges (see pages 56 and 57 for examples).
- Even if the different aspects of the personality cannot be identified or measured, they are still helpful in understanding the human experience, for instance in relationships where harsh parenting can cause someone to often feel guilty because they have acquired a strong Superego.
- This model can be seen as complete because it encompasses the influences of instinct (biological), logic (cognitive) and other people (social).

Freud: defence mechanisms

- Defence mechanisms are ways that the unconscious hides thoughts from consciousness.
- They serve to protect us from being aware of painful or guilty thoughts, feelings or desires.

defence mechanism	definition	example
repression	recall of an unpleasant memory or the emotion associated with it is unconsciously blocked	being unable to remember the last few moments before a car accident
displacement	emotions are redirected from the individual who caused them to a different person or object	coming home and shouting at the dog because you've had a bad day at school
reaction formation	adopting an attitude that is the direct opposite of our genuine feelings	a girl is overly pleasant to someone who bullied her years before
denial	refusal to accept that events are happening or have happened	an alcoholic refuses to admit that they have a drink problem
projection	shifting our own undesirable characteristics or feelings to someone else, so alleviating blame	a lad who is keen for a fight shouts 'What's your problem pal? Looking for a fight?' to an innocent stranger
regression	behaving in a comforting, child-like way when under emotional pressure	a examination candidate sucks their thumb

Adams et al. (1996)

Aim: to see if homophobic men were aroused by gay porn to test for reaction formation.

Procedure: 35 homophobic and 29 non-homophobic men were shown explicit videos of gay, lesbian and heterosexual sex. Physiological measures of sexual arousal were taken for each video type. The men also estimated how aroused they felt in each category of video. In addition they completed a questionnaire to measure aggression. The two groups were compared on their aggression and arousal (as measured physiologically and by self-report).

Findings: no difference was found in aggression between the groups nor was there a difference in arousal while watching lesbian or heterosexual scenes. However, 80% of homophobic men, but only 33% of non-homophobic men, were aroused by the gay scenes. The homophobic group under-estimated their response to gay scenes.

Conclusion: reaction formation – a defence against a fear of being gay – may be responsible for homophobic attitudes.

strengths of defence mechanisms

- Evidence from case studies (e.g. Freud, 1905 – see page 57) supports the idea.
- Experimental evidence also supports the existence of defence mechanisms, e.g. Adams et al. (see below) and Koehler et al. (2002) who found that for people learning word lists, words which caused greater anxiety were more likely to be forgotten, suggesting that they were being repressed.

weaknesses of defence mechanisms

- Defence mechanisms are difficult to test objectively because they are unconscious and because it is unethical to artificially induce traumatic situations.
- Forgetting may occur for reasons other than defence mechanisms and, once a memory has been lost, it is difficult to determine the cause.

Freud: psychosexual stages of development

- Freud (1905) suggested that children pass through stages of development because the focus of their libido changes.
- The *libido* (a positive force) becomes the sexual energy of adulthood but in childhood it manifests itself as pleasure from different organs with associated characteristics.
- Each stage has a developmental task.
- If a trauma occurs, the child may become fixated at that stage, retaining the related personality characteristics into adulthood.
- In the oral stage, the child is dependent, it needs others for food and comfort. A trauma at this stage can cause the person to retain these characteristics.
- In the anal stage, children become aware of their own desires, and conflicts can arise when others impose restrictions, such as insisting on potty training. If this is done harshly and anal fixation occurs, the individual's adult personality will be dominated by the conflicts of the anal stage, e.g. being orderly.

strengths of Adams et al. (1996)

As a laboratory experiment, it had good controls:
- the baseline test of aggression showed that the homophobic men were no more violent;
- arousal to different stimuli was compared;
- two measures of arousal were used to see whether the response was unconscious.

weaknesses of Adams et al. (1996)

- The self-report measures of arousal, aggression and homophobia could have been affected by social desirability as homophobia is a socially sensitive issue.
- Measuring sexual arousal is invasive so the willing sample may have been biased.

Freud: psychosexual development

stage	age (years)	developmental task	organ of pleasure	effects of fixation
oral	0–1	weaning	mouth	smoker, greedy, passive, dependent, gullible
anal	2–3	potty training	anus	very tidy or untidy, mean, obstinate
phallic	3–6	Oedipus complex	genitals	being reckless or overly careful
latency	6–12	development of defence mechanisms	Freud believed that the libido was quiescent. As there is no organ of pleasure there can be no fixation	
genital	12–18	developing mature sexual relationships	genitals	If early stages have been achieved, adults should achieve successful sexual maturity

strengths of psychosexual development

- Evidence suggests that the quality of the relationship between a child and its carers, e.g. separation, can have lasting effects.
- Evidence supports some personality types, e.g. O'Neill et al. (1992) found a link between anal personality and enjoyment of 'toilet humour'.

weaknesses of psychosexual development

- Psychosexuality operates unconsciously so is hard to investigate objectively.
- Evidence suggests that the Oedipal conflict is not central to psychological development. Golombok (2000) found no evidence for deficient development in children in single or same-sex parent families compared to two-parent heterosexual ones (which Freud would have predicted, as the Oedipal conflict could not arise in either of the former).

Freud: the Oedipus complex

Freud suggested that, during the phallic stage, the child becomes fully aware of its own gender and notices that it is excluded from aspects of its parents' lives, e.g. sleeping in the same room. The three-way relationship between mother, father and child is called the Oedipus complex. Freud suggested that rivalry exists between the child and the same sex parent for the attention of the opposite sex parent. The child resents its exclusion because, unconsciously, it has sexual and destructive desires. The task of the phallic stage is to resolve this conflict. Failure to do so would cause fixation and a corresponding adult personality.

Freud (1905): little Hans

Aim: to interpret a 5-year-old boy's phobia.

Procedure: information about the boy, Hans, came mainly from Hans' father in weekly reports and a description of Hans' early life.

Findings: from age 3, Hans was interested in his penis. Several things happened:

- Hans' mother threatened to cut off his penis if he didn't stop playing with it.
- Hans' father objected to Hans getting into bed with his parents.
- Hans developed a phobia of horses, fearing that they would bite him.

Hans' fear seemed to be linked to the horse's large penis. The phobia worsened and Hans was unwilling to go out in case he met a horse. The phobia then improved, relating only to horses with black harnesses over their noses, which Hans' father interpreted as his own moustache. The end of the phobia coincided with two fantasies. In one, he had imaginary children. When asked who their mother was, Hans said 'mummy, and you're their grandaddy'. In the second, a plumber fitted him with a bigger penis.

Conclusion: Freud's interpretation was that Hans' fear of horses related to the Oedipus complex, symbolising his fear of his father (because they had black harnesses and big penises). The conflict arose over access to the parents' bed as this allowed Hans' father, but not Hans, access to his mother. Freud believed that Hans resolved this conflict as he fantasised himself with a big penis, married to his mother.

strengths of Freud (1905)

- The case study allowed detailed data to be collected so a range of information, such as descriptions of fears, wishes and fantasies, could be gathered and interpreted.
- Freud's case studies, such as this, led to the useful application of psychotherapy which is still used to treat people effectively.

weaknesses of Freud (1905)

- The data was not obtained directly from Hans and Hans' father could have been biased by their relationship.
- Hans' father may have lacked objectivity as he knew Freud, so would have been aware of his ideas, e.g. the Oedipus complex.

Freud: dream theory

The function of dreams, according to Freud, is the fulfilment of unconscious wishes. He described dreams as having two levels:

- *manifest content* – the 'storyline' we are consciously aware of that contains symbols;
- *latent content* – the underlying wishes, or meaning, of the dream that can be discovered by interpreting the symbols reported in the manifest content.

Dreamwork translates the wishes into the manifest content, hiding the real meaning of a dream from conscious recall, protecting us from anxiety and allowing us to sleep undisturbed.

Not all dreams are symbolic, some are simply expressions of wishes or thoughts that are not unpleasant so do not need to be disguised.

Three processes occur in dreamwork:

- *displacement* – where an object or person that is causing distress is replaced by another, e.g. dreaming about killing a dog when 'dog' is the way you refer to a person you hate. The dream represents the desire to kill the loathsome person;
- *condensation* – where several aspects of a situation are combined (or 'condensed') into one, e.g. the punishing of one man symbolising a woman's anger towards her father and husband;
- *secondary elaboration* – where the symbols in the dream are further disguised by making them into a story-like sequence.

Freud was cautious about the idea of universal symbols, suggesting instead that symbols were unique to the individual.

comparing dream theories: Freud and Hobson & McCarley

See page 70 for a description of Hobson & McCarley and note the exam hint.

	Freud	Hobson & McCarley
reason for dreaming	wish fulfilment	just random activation of neurones
use of symbols in dreams	yes	no
explanation for 'storyline' in dreams	secondary elaboration to further hide the latent content	synthesis of the randomly activated memories
explanation for recurrent dreams	unsolved unconscious dilemma	difficult to explain
meaning of dreams	reveal hidden fears and wishes	no meaning
evidence	case studies (e.g. Freud, 1905) and some physiological evidence (e.g, Solms, 2000)	physiological evidence, e.g. Hobson & McCarley, 1977
reliability	low, as case studies may be interpreted in different ways	high, as experimental evidence can be replicated
explanation for dreaming of recent events	relate to recent thoughts and wishes which are not hidden	difficult to explain

'I dreamt about running down a grey-haired woman in my car.'

'That means you want to kill our Maths teacher, Mrs Bones, because she gave you a fail in the last test.'

'No, it doesn't. It's just because your driving test is next week and you had that near miss with an old lady yesterday.'

strengths of dream theory

- This theory can explain recurrent dreams, as the wishes may remain unfulfilled so can reappear.
- Dreams often reflect our conscious worries, suggesting that they relate to unconscious conflicts.
- The interpretation of a dream is often acceptable to the dreamer, suggesting symbols can be understood and may be plausible and helpful.
- The theory is supported by physiological evidence, e.g. Solms (2000) who found that damage to one brain region affected both dreaming and wishing, suggesting they are linked as Freud proposed.

weaknesses of dream theory

- Hobson & McCarley (see page 70) found physiological evidence that dreams were caused by the random firing of neurones so cannot be related to specific wishes.
- Analysis of symbols in dreams is subjective (see page 60) so interpretations cannot be verified.

Erikson (1959): theory of lifespan development

In contrast to Freud's idea that personality was determined in early childhood, Erikson suggested that, although childhood was important, the personality continued to develop throughout life. He shared with Freud a belief in the importance of the Ego and divided the lifespan into eight *psychosocial stages*, through which the individual must pass. Each stage is characterised by a crisis or conflict and it is overcoming these that develops the Ego because it enables the individual to achieve a developmental task.

These work towards the formation of a balanced, individual identity of the self in society. Unlike Freud, Erikson believed that an individual could still progress even if the conflict was only partially resolved, i.e. fixation would not occur. As a result, there are characteristics of both resolution, and failure to resolve each crisis. He also differed in suggesting that social and cultural factors were important in development, as well as the influence of the immediate family.

life stage	age (years)	conflict to be resolved	description of conflict	developmental task
early infancy	0–1	trust v. mistrust	balance of trusting people and risking being let down or being suspicious and not socialising	to develop a sense of trust
later infancy	1–3	autonomy v. shame and doubt	developing a sense of control over oneself or not being in control and anticipating failure	to establish an independent identity
early childhood	4–6	initiative v. guilt	gain personal responsibility or feel guilty or ashamed	to feel free to explore the world
middle childhood	7–12	industry v. inferiority	learn to work for success (e.g. physical or academic) or avoid challenges and feel inferior	to be busy in order to learn to achieve
puberty and adolescence	13–18	identity v. role confusion	reach a sense of personal and social identity or be bewildered by choices and expectations	to develop an adult social and sexual identity
young adulthood	19–25	intimacy v. isolation	have close, trusting relationships or avoid them to escape threat and pain	to establish healthy adult relationships
mature adulthood	26–40s	generativity v. stagnation	achieve and be productive (e.g. in work or society) or stagnate and fail to move forwards	to surrender youth and focus on the next generation
late adulthood	50s+	integrity v. despair	look back on life positively or feel that life has been meaningless and not worthwhile	to accept one's own life and impending death

strengths of Erikson

- Because the theory describes changes over the whole lifespan, it provides a greater understanding of adulthood than Freud's theory.
- By studying other cultures and considering the role of culture in development, Erikson's theory is less culture-bound.
- This theory is more testable than Freud's and there is evidence such as McAdams et al. (1997) who showed that generative adults were more prosocial and optimistic suggesting that generativity is related to moving forward positively, i.e. Ego development.
- It can be used to understand adult mental health problems, i.e. has applications (see page 61).

Freud and Erikson: similarities and differences

	Freud	Erikson
duration of personality development	early childhood	over whole lifespan
number of stages	5	8
characteristics of stages	libido focused on one organ	crisis to be resolved
existence of Id, Ego and Superego	yes	yes
important influences	parents	parents, society, culture
effect of negative experiences	fixation and related adult personality	conflict remains unresolved

weaknesses of Erikson

- The stages are quite rigid so fail to account for individual differences but particular experiences (e.g. a bereavement) are likely to be more important than predetermined conflicts at any age.
- Erikson's research was based on data from men, but the conclusions were applied to women. The developmental needs of women, however, may be different, e.g. the desire to form nurturing relationships during adolescence rather than focusing on the formation of a separate identity.

strengths of case studies of people in therapy

- They generate rich, in-depth data because the individual is allowed to talk freely so provides more detailed information than would be gained in an experiment.

- They allow researchers to look at the way many factors may be involved in a complex situation, such as the role of individual differences in development or family dynamics and trauma on later behaviour.

case studies of people in therapy

- Case studies are detailed, descriptive investigations.

- They investigate a single instance, for example one person or family.

- Case studies may utilise other techniques, such as interviews or observations.

- The client is listened to while they talk about their past experiences and their current problems.

- The researcher or analyst then interprets the comments in order to understand the relationships between their problems and previous events.

weaknesses of case studies of people in therapy

- The researcher may lack objectivity if they get to know the individual well.

- The researcher may be subjective, e.g. if they have a particular theoretical bias. This reduces validity.

- Results are unlikely to generalise to other people because no two people's experiences or problems are identical.

strengths of clinical interviews

- By waiting for clients to show resistance, analysts may be able to identify the appearance of unconscious thoughts, which are difficult to access by other methods.

- Uninterrupted listening allows the analyst to gather valid data about the client's experiences and feelings.

clinical interviews

- Face-to-face questions are asked by an analyst to a client.

- The analyst listens carefully to the responses, organising and interpreting them.

- The analyst can prompt the client by asking particular questions but does not direct the topics.

- The intention is for the client to talk in an unrestricted way to reveal unconscious thoughts and wishes.

weaknesses of clinical interviews

- People's recall of their early childhood is often inaccurate and symptoms such as depression may cause more negative recollections of the past which further distorts the client's perception.

- Interviewers may be subjective and, because interview questions can differ, comparison and generalisation are difficult.

strengths of analysis of symbols

- Freud identified symbolism as characteristic of the unconscious mind, so the analysis of symbols is the only effective route to understanding hidden anxieties or motives.

- It is useful as the content of recurrent (and other) dreams and reoccurring themes in films can be explained.

analysis of symbols

- Dreams and slips of the tongue are sources of symbols, as well as films and literature.

- Symbols are representations of unconscious thoughts that appear in a different form in conscious thoughts or behaviours; e.g. in dreams the manifest content (what we remember) symbolises the latent (unconscious) content.

- The symbols are interpreted by the researcher to reveal unconscious motives, fears or desires.

- Freud was cautious about the idea of universal symbols, suggesting instead that symbols were unique to the individual.

weaknesses of analysis of symbols

- Interpretation of symbols is subjective. Different analysts may conclude different meanings (if any) for the same symbols.

- Interpretation cannot be objectively verified.

- The content of dreams may be more effectively explained by other theories, such as the random activation of recent memories.

Lemma-Wright (1995): Alex: a case of childhood trauma

This case describes Alex who loved her younger sister as a child. Alex also resented the attention her sister received and once dragged her into the sea because it made her angry. In adulthood, Alex felt obliged to help her sister. One birthday, she organised a boat trip for her sister and suffered a panic attack on board. Later Alex dreamt of fighting with a friend and wishing her dead. The friend reminded Alex of her sister and she realised that, on the boat trip, she had taken her sister back into the sea, bringing back guilty memories of dragging her into the sea when they were children.

The interpretation shows how childhood memories can appear to produce anxiety, manifesting as a panic attack. Here, as the psychodynamic approach suggests, early experiences with relationships caused unconscious feelings that affected later emotions. This understanding, in turn, could help to overcome the consequent symptoms. However, although we have reports of her childhood feelings, the dream and her symptoms of panic, there is nothing to say that they are related.

applying the psychodynamic approach to mental health

Psychodynamic theories rely on the effects of the unconscious and early experience. Unconscious conflicts can manifest as symptoms of mental disorder, and problems with early relationships, whether conscious or unconscious, can affect later mental health.

Brown & Harris (1978)

Aim: to investigate a link between early stress and later depression.

Procedure: 539 women in Camberwell, London were interviewed to find out about recent and childhood stress and the reports were rated by independent researchers for stressfulness. Later, information about whether each women was depressed was obtained.

Findings: although recent stressors were very important, childhood stress, particularly the death of the mother before the age of 11, was also associated with later depression.

Conclusion: depression in adulthood is related to early trauma.

Freud and mental health

Childhood trauma can disrupt psychosexual development, causing fixation which can lead to mental health problems because the wishes or desires of that stage are repressed. For example, fixation at the oral stage may cause eating disorders or increase the risk of addiction ('dependent' type behaviours), whereas fixation at the anal stage may cause obsessive-compulsive disorders (relating to the need to be 'orderly' and clean).

Erikson and mental health

At each stage, failure to overcome the crisis has the potential to cause problems. For example, in mature adulthood there is a need for generativity – to feel that a contribution is being made to the next generation. If this is not achieved, the individual may become depressed. Erikson's theory suggests ways other than bearing children in which this crisis may be resolved.

strengths of psychodynamic explanations of mental health

- Psychodynamic explanations are supported by evidence such as Eley & Stevenson (2000) who found a link between early frightening experiences and later anxiety disorders (although they also found a genetic component) and Brown & Harris (1978) – see above.
- See also psychodynamic explanation of phobia, page 57.
- Erikson's theory can offer alternative ways to resolve adult crises to help people whose development has stalled.
- The psychodynamic approach led to psychotherapy which uses techniques such as interpretation of dreams and defences to identify unconscious conflicts which are responsible for mental health problems.
- Evidence shows that psychotherapy is effective for people with mental health problems, e.g. Sandell (1999) found a reduction of symptoms in patients over three years.

weaknesses of psychodynamic explanations of mental health

- There is good evidence that unconscious factors are not the only important ones in mental health problems. Genetic factors and learning are also important (e.g. Eley & Stevenson).
- Because the explanations are based on unconscious fears or wishes that are difficult to study, the ideas are hard to verify.

Schlozman: vampires and those who slay them

an Eriksonian perspective

Psychodynamic theory helps us to understand an audience's attraction to vampires. Schlozman suggests that the characteristics of vampires, such as power, strength, immaturity, emptiness and lack of fulfilment are symbolic of the *unresolved conflicts* suffered by adolescents as described by Erikson. The trials experienced by Buffy depict the challenges faced by young people trying to resolve the conflict of *identity versus role confusion* as she wrestles with academic, social and sexual issues. The plot allows her to express both vulnerability and power – she therefore illustrates the strength to negotiate her way through the guilt and dilemmas of adolescence.

- The conflict experienced by adolescents confronting their sexual identity is symbolised by the obsessional love between Buffy, a slayer, and Angel, a vampire, who subsists on animal blood from the butcher.

- The intensity of the vampire's need for biting necks and sucking blood symbolises the adolescents' aggressive and sexual feelings as they search for their identity.

- Once bitten, a vampire's victim becomes the vampire – so the identity crisis is overcome by displacement.

- Erikson, unlike Freud, identified a role for the influence of the family throughout development. Giles takes on a 'paternal' role following the divorce of Buffy's parents and he helps to guide her through the maze of adolescence.

why we watch *Buffy*: is it a contemporary issue?

Buffy the Vampire Slayer has a cult following, which psychodynamic psychology can help us to explain.

The characters and plot

Fifteen-year-old high school cheerleader Buffy discovers that she, as the 'chosen one', has been given superhuman powers to fight evil: she is a 'slayer'. She learns to slay vampires under the guidance of Giles her school librarian (who becomes her 'surrogate father') and continues life at school and home. The cast includes Buffy's friends Willow and Xander, Willow's boyfriend Oz – a werewolf – and later Buffy's lover Angel (a vampire 'reformed' by a curse).

Schlozman (2000): vampires and those who slay them

Schlozman has explored details of *Buffy the Vampire Slayer*, identifying and interpreting characters and events from a psychodynamic perspective and describing the unconscious fears and desires that they may symbolise.

Schlozman: vampires and those who slay them

a Freudian perspective

Unconscious fears are, according to Freud, disguised by *defence mechanisms* in order to protect the conscious mind. Skal (1993) suggests that we enjoy horror stories (e.g. in films or on television) because they symbolise our fears so we can safely *displace* our anxiety onto them. For example, we fear death but we cannot confront this fear directly. Instead we gain unconscious relief from seeing Buffy slaying a vampire and symbolising the defeat of death.

The fears surrounding sex for Angel (about consuming Buffy) and Buffy (about falling into the vampire world) symbolise *repressed* adolescent fears about intimate and sexual relationships in the real world.

how convincing is this evidence?

- Evidence from studies such as Schlozman's represent one possible interpretation. Since this cannot be objectively verified, other interpretations could equally be correct.

- Other evidence (such as Skal, 1993) suggests that cultural trends, in addition to individual crises, influence our unconscious preferences within the horror genre. If Schlozman's interpretation is correct, Buffy should have enduring appeal – especially for adolescents – but it also attracts an adult audience and only longitudinal evidence will show whether it will last.

theories

- The two sides of the balance in the illustration are like your Id and Ego, competing for control. Which is driven by the pleasure principle and which by the morality principle? Which part of the mind 'balances' these two?
- Outline **one** psychodynamic theory **other** than Freud's.
- Evaluate this theory in terms of its strengths and weaknesses.
- Freud proposed an explanation for the function of dreams. Describe this theory of dreaming.
- How did Freud explain the tendency to forget dreams so quickly?
- Identify **two** criticisms of this theory.
- Explain what is meant by a 'defence mechanism'?
- How do defence mechanisms help us?
- Identify as many different defence mechanisms as you can from the central box below. Name and define each defence mechanism that you have identified, explaining how it links to the text.

studies

- Identify **two** studies from the psychodynamic approach.
- Describe the procedure and conclusion of **one** of these studies.
- Outline **two** criticisms of the study you have described.

general assumptions

One general assumption from the psychodynamic approach is the importance of early experience.

- Explain why early experiences can affect our adult life.
- The case of Alex is an example of a woman who feels obliged to help her sister as an adult because she tried to harm her as a child. How do Alex's feelings relate to this general assumption?

application

Theories from the psychodynamic approach have been used to understand mental health issues.

- Name at least **one** mental health problem.
- Identify **two** theories from the psychodynamic approach.
- Explain how each of the psychodynamic theories would account for the symptom(s).

defence mechanisms

Gordon was a successful businessman but there is now a risk that his business might fail. This is in part because Gordon sent some very rude letters to his most important clients when they harassed him about a late delivery.

Even though there is virtually no work, Gordon stays late at the office, tidying his desk and moving files around, believing he is busy. He suspects that the decline in sales relates to something he did, but he has no recollection of doing anything wrong. When everyone else has gone home, Gordon stops drinking tea and coffee, takes a bottle of milk out of the fridge and makes himself a glass of warm milk in the microwave. When he goes home, he tells his wife how worried he is about the state of their roof – even though there is nothing wrong with it.

research methods

Gordon keeps having strange dreams and decides to see a psychotherapist to find out if they mean anything. During the consultation, the therapist asks him questions and listens intently while Gordon answers. He interprets Gordon's replies and his descriptions of his dreams.

- One method used in the psychodynamic approach is the case study. **Two** other methods commonly used in this approach are described above, identify them.
- Describe **two** strengths and **two** weaknesses of each of these methods.

contemporary issue

Many films, books and TV programmes, for example *Buffy the Vampire Slayer*, feature monsters. The psychodynamic approach has been used to interpret their characters and plot lines.

- Use your understanding of psychodynamic theories and concepts to explain why people are attracted to one or more named examples of such sources of entertainment.

theories

- Describe the stages of psychosexual development according to Freud.
- Define the term 'fixation'.
- Apply the theory of psychosexual development to Dennis.
  - At which stage do you think Dennis could fixate, and why?
  - If Dennis's father recovered fully and returned home after many months, explain how Dennis might respond.
- Describe **two** strengths and **two** weaknesses of the stage theory of psychosexual development.

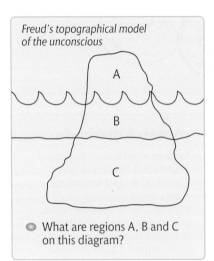

Freud's topographical model of the unconscious

- What are regions A, B and C on this diagram?

studies

- Identify **one** study from the psychodynamic approach.
- Identify the research method that it uses.
- Evaluate the study you have identified in terms of **two** strengths and **two** weaknesses.

psychosexual development

A small boy, Dennis, lives with his mum and dad. He was a happy baby, feeding from the breast and weaning without distress at 13 months. He doesn't suck his thumb, although he has an old toy dog he drags around everywhere and chews occasionally.

Dennis is now 3 years old and his dad has had to go into hospital. His mum doesn't want to leave Dennis with anyone else so takes him to the hospital every night to visit his father. The hospital smells strange to Dennis, his father looks different and doesn't smile. His mum cries a lot and when Dennis, who is just out of nappies, messes in his pants for the third evening in a row, his mum really shouts at him. Dennis cries and is told he won't be allowed to come again because he is disturbing other patients.

contemporary issue

Post Traumatic Stress Disorder (PTSD) is increasingly common as people are exposed to mass tragedies such as rail crashes and school killings. Many of the sufferers show a range of symptoms. These include:

- being unable to remember the incident or events immediately before or after it;
- being unpredictably aggressive towards other people;
- crying and huddling up in a foetal position every time they think about it;
- having strange dreams.

Use your knowledge of the studies and theories from the psychodynamic approach to explain how these symptoms, and other problems caused by a traumatic incident, could arise.

general assumptions

One general assumption from the psychodynamic approach is 'the importance of the unconscious mind'.

- Describe **two** aspects of the unconscious mind.
- Outline **two** ways in which the unconscious mind could affect our behaviour, thinking or feelings.

research methods

- Much research in the psychodynamic approach uses the case study. Describe this method of collecting data.
- Explain why the case study is particularly suited to use in the psychodynamic approach.
- Identify and describe **one** ethical issue that can arise in case studies in the psychodynamic approach.

application

The psychodynamic approach can be used to help us to understand mental health issues.

- Outline **two** concepts from the psychodynamic approach that could be used to understand mental health issues.
- Illustrate **one** of these concepts with an example of a mental health issue and explain how the issue would be accounted for.

chapter 6

the physiological approach

what you need to know   66

general assumptions   67

EEGs and sleep stages   68

theories of sleep   69

theory of dreaming   70

research methods   71

studies in detail   73

circadian rhythms   74

application   75

contemporary issue   76

questions   77

the physiological approach

Physiological psychology looks at the biological causes of emotion, cognition and behaviour, for instance the way that genes determine personality, and the brain controls the daily sleep cycle.

what's it about?

general assumptions

You need to understand and be able to describe at least **two** general assumptions of the physiological approach:

- the **importance of genetic influences** – how they control individual differences;
- the **importance of the nervous system** – its role in psychological processes such as emotion, cognition and behaviour.

theories

in-depth areas of study

You need to be able to describe:

- **circadian rhythms**;
- research into the day/night cycle including the influence of:
  - endogenous pacemakers;
  - zeitgebers;
- the relationship between EEG criteria and **sleep stages**.

You also need to be able to describe and evaluate:

- **restoration theory of sleep**;
- one other theory of sleep, e.g. **evolutionary theory**;
- one physiological theory of dreaming, e.g. **activation-synthesis**.

You will also need to be able to apply these theories to situations for the key application and contemporary issue.

classic research / research now

studies in detail

You need to be able to identify, describe and evaluate in detail **two** studies from the physiological approach, e.g.

- **Dement & Kleitman (1957)** – used EEGs to monitor sleep stages to relate eye movements to dream content;
- **Heston (1966)** – a correlational study that investigated the heritability of schizophrenia.

research methods

methods

You need to be able to outline and discuss research methods commonly used in the physiological approach including:

- ways to study the brain:
  - **brain scanning**;
  - **EEG**;
  - **lesioning**;
- ways to study genetic influences on individual differences:
  - **correlational techniques**, e.g. twin and adoption studies.

It is helpful if you can also remember an example of each of these methods being used in physiological psychology: Maguire et al. (1997) used brain scanning to investigate the role of the hippocampus in navigation; Aserinsky & Kleitman (1953) used EEGs to monitor sleep stages; Ralph et al. (1990) investigated the role of the SCN using lesioning; and Heston (1966) conducted an adoption study.

You also need to be able to show how EEG criteria relate to sleep stages.

real lives

key application

You need to be able to understand and discuss links between physiological concepts including circadian rhythms and the effects of:

- shift work;
- jet lag.

To do this, you should be able to use concepts and research from physiological psychology to explain the cause of the problems that arise and to understand strategies for overcoming these problems.

talking point

contemporary issue

You will need to use your knowledge of the physiological approach to explain a current issue, e.g. **lucid dreaming**.

For this, you will need to:
- be able to describe the issue;
- use **at least one concept** from the learning approach to explain the issue (e.g. using EEGs and/or the conflict or support lucid dreaming offers for theories of sleep and dreaming);
- use terminology from the physiological approach.

You can also be asked to apply the concepts to a contemporary issue you have *not* studied.

the importance of genetic influences

genetic influences and psychology

- We each inherit a unique combination of genes from our parents (except identical twins, who are genetically the same).
- 50% comes from the mother, 50% from the father.
- These genes are important in determining our individual characteristics such as personality, abilities and behaviour.
- The effects of genes can be seen in physical abilities such as being able or unable to roll your tongue.

This is important because:

- although single genes can control individual characteristics (such as being able to roll your tongue), this is unusual for psychological variables;
- in general, psychological variables are the product of a combination of genes or the interaction of genes and the environment;
- understanding the relative influence of genes and the environment can help us to identify the potential influences on mental health, e.g. in schizophrenia.

the importance of the nervous system

the nervous system and psychology

- The major biological influence on our behaviour, cognitions and emotions is our nervous system (consisting of the brain, spinal cord and body nerves).
- It is made up of special cells called neurones, specialised for communication within the body. Messages are electrical within neurones but chemical between them.
- The nervous system receives external information and triggers behaviours.
- The brain controls many different functions. It has specialised areas for many of these, e.g. memory, vision and the control of sleep.
- The nervous system interacts with other parts of the body and controls them, e.g. stimulating the release of hormones from glands.

This is important because:

- understanding the normal function of the brain, such as how it controls sleep, can be useful in minimising problems for individuals, such as when their sleep patterns are disturbed by shift working or jet lag;
- knowing about the role of different brain areas can help us to understand when things go wrong with behaviour or cognition, e.g. when hippocampal damage causes memory loss;
- knowing how the messages in neurones are conducted allows us to monitor the brain. This helps to find out about normal and abnormal processes using electrical techniques;
- we can understand the effects of drugs as they act like chemicals normally present within the nervous system.

what is sleep?

- Sleep is a necessary state of altered consciousness experienced by animals with a central nervous system.
- It is rhythmical and characterised by reduced sensory and motor function.

rapid-eye-movement sleep (REM)

- The EEG for REM sleep is most similar to being awake.
- The sleeper is paralysed.
- The sleeper's eyes move rapidly under their eyelids.
- When woken during REM sleep individuals generally report that they were dreaming.

non-rapid-eye-movement sleep (nREM)

- Stages 1–4 (see below) are nREM sleep.
- The sleeper does not have rapid eye movements and their body is not paralysed (they can turn over easily and some people may sleep walk).
- The deeper the sleep (i.e. towards stage 4,) the harder the sleeper is to wake up.
- Generally, when sleepers are awoken from nREM sleep, they do not report visual, vivid dreams (although they may say they were 'thinking').

how is sleep studied?

- Changes in brain activity are detected by an EEG. The patterns are consistent between individuals and are therefore useful.
- The effects of brain areas on sleep patterns can be studied by lesioning.
- The frequency but not the direction of rapid eye movements (REM) during sleep can be recorded using an EOG (electrooculogram).
- Muscle activity during sleep can be monitored using an EMG (electromyogram).

sleep stages

Aserinsky & Kleitman (1953) recorded the brain activity (EEG) and eye movements of sleeping participants. They found consistent patterns in a night's sleep:

- People generally fall into stage 1 sleep.
- Sleep becomes deeper through stages 2, 3 and 4 (these are nREM stages).
- Sleep then becomes lighter again through stage 3, then 2.
- The sleeper then enters a phase of REM sleep (rather than re-entering stage 1) before returning to stage 2.
- The sleeper continues to cycle through the stages about every 90 minutes during the night but:
  - REM phases become longer;
  - less deep sleep occurs with each cycle.
- Finally, natural waking tends to occur in REM.

The 90 minute cycles are *ultradian rhythms*.

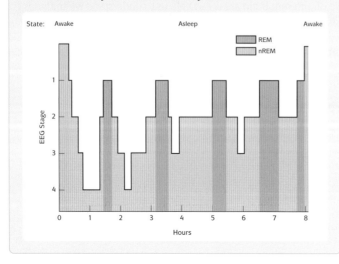

EEG recordings: brain wave patterns in sleep and waking

- Both waking and REM sleep have low amplitude, high frequency beta waves characteristic of active thinking.
- Deep sleep (i.e. stage 4) has high amplitude, low frequency delta waves.
- Stage 2 sleep has spindles (short bursts of high frequency waves) and K complexes (sudden high amplitude waves).

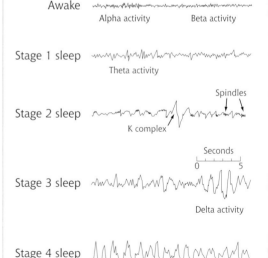

strengths of evolutionary theory

- Evidence supports the influence of evolution on sleep as more similar animals have more similar stages. For example, birds and mammals have both REM and nREM sleep, but some reptiles (to which we are less closely related) have only REM sleep.

- The patterns of sleep seen in different species, such as desert animals sleeping during the day, fit with the widely accepted ideas of evolution as 'survival of the fittest' – by keeping safe when they are at risk.

evolutionary theory of sleep

Meddis (1977) suggests that, since sleep has evolved, it must help animals to survive. Species that have different survival needs would therefore have evolved different sleep patterns. The characteristics of sleep in humans must also be adaptive, or have been so in our evolutionary history. Sleeping may not seem like a behaviour that helps survival – being less likely to detect danger and less able to move would be detrimental to escape responses from predators, for example. But, if an animal is asleep, it is still and quiet – a good way to hide from predators. So animals not well suited to survival at certain times of day, such as in darkness when they cannot see, would benefit from keeping 'out of trouble'. Similarly, those poorly adapted to survival in the midday heat or night-time cold would gain from being asleep at these times.

weaknesses of evolutionary theory

- There are many aspects of sleep that this theory cannot explain, such as the patterns within sleep.

- It seems unlikely that 'doing nothing' is the best evolutionary strategy. Therefore other theories, that suggest more practical benefits for sleep, such as restoration, are more probable.

- Sleeping is essential and cannot be avoided. For example, an individual deprived of sleep eventually succumbs. Similarly, sleep still occurs in animals for whom the state is potentially maladaptive (such as diving mammals which might drown). These observations suggest that there is a more essential reason for sleeping.

sleep

Sleep is a lowered state of consciousness typified by reduced movement and sensitivity to our environment.

strengths of restorational theory

There is evidence for replenishing energy during sleep:

- The body uses energy in the form of ATP. During sleep we use only two-thirds of the energy we use even whilst at rest and ATP levels are higher during sleep than wakefulness, supporting restorational theory.

- During REM we are paralysed and this may be important for recuperation of muscles as heavier people (whose muscles have to work harder) spend longer in REM sleep.

- Greater time is spent asleep following vigorous exercise which also supports the need for restoration of energy and muscles.

There is evidence for repair during sleep:

- Rechtschaffen et al. (1983) showed that animals deprived of sleep become sick, suggesting that sleep is needed for maintaining health.

There is evidence for growth during sleep:

- Growth hormone is naturally released during deep sleep and, when used artificially to stimulate growth, it is more effective at night than in the morning.

restorational theory of sleep

Oswald (1969) proposed that sleep was necessary for physiological recovery from the day: a time for growth, repair and replenishment of energy. It makes sense to stop using systems in order to maintain them – you can't drive a car and refuel or repair it simultaneously.

Do we need more sleep to restore ourselves after physical exercise?

weaknesses of restorational theory

- Evidence linking weight and time in REM sleep is correlational so there could be reasons that explain the increase in sleep other than the need for restoration.

- Extra exercise causes longer sleep but resting does not result in less sleeping, suggesting that energy restoration is not a complete explanation.

- Dreaming uses energy which contradicts the idea of conserving it.

strengths of activation-synthesis theory

- Physiological evidence supports the existence of auto-activation. Neurones called giant cells start a wave of activity (the PGO wave) that results in stimulation of brain areas responsible for eye movements, vision, physical movement and memory. This accounts for the existence of REMs, and for the appearance of sights and movements in the content of dreams.

- This theory explains many aspects of dreams such as their bizarre content, resulting from the random activation of different memories in the cortex – and their story-like nature – because we tend to organise memories in coherent ways.

dreams

Dreaming occurs predominantly in REM sleep and consists of imaginary but vivid, generally visual sequences that may be recalled for a short period upon waking but then fade from memory unless rehearsed.

activation-synthesis theory of dreaming

Hobson & McCarley (1977) proposed that dreams were the result of the *random* 'auto-activation' of the brain, that is, the brain triggering its own activity rather than responding to external stimuli.

They suggested that signals starting in the brain stem (called PGO waves, see diagram) triggered *activation*, that is, neural activity. This activity spreads, especially to regions of the cortex such as the occipital lobe (for vision), motor areas and auditory areas. The brain then interprets the internally generated signals as if they had originated externally. This process, using memories to make sense of the activation and create a 'story', is called *synthesis* and results in a sequence that we recall as a dream. During this process the brain is isolated from incoming sensory information and is prevented from sending out instructions to move. This is necessary otherwise we might 'act out' our dreams.

weaknesses of activation-synthesis theory

- There is physiological evidence for the involvement of more brain areas in dreaming than Hobson & McCarley envisaged, suggesting that their theory is an incomplete explanation.

- If activation was, as Hobson & McCarley suggested, entirely random then dream content should be too. However, we often dream about recent events, some people have recurring dreams and many people feel that dreams are meaningful which would not be the case if the content was randomly generated.

PGO waves start in the **p**ontine reticular formation, pass to the **g**eniculate nucleus and then to the **o**ccipital lobe (see diagram).

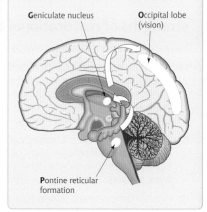

Geniculate nucleus   **O**ccipital lobe (vision)

Pontine reticular formation

exam note

In this section it is easy to get muddled. Try to remember the following points:

- Look for the difference between questions about 'sleep' and questions about 'dreaming' – they are not asking you the same thing!

- There is more overlap between what you need to know for 'in-depth areas of study', theories, studies, research methods and applications than you will find in many other approaches. For example, *EEGs* appear in methods and in-depth areas of study, and *circadian rhythms* appear in in-depth areas of study and applications. Don't be afraid to use this material in different contexts.

- It is easy to muddle up your **physiological** theory of dreaming and Freud's theory of dreams (from the **psychodynamic** approach) as they both appear on the Unit 2 exam. If you answer a question about dreaming, *make sure* you have read the question correctly.

strengths of lesioning

- More informative than studying the effects of brain damage through autopsies as consequent behaviour can be observed.
- Controlled surgery on animals is exact so offers greater confidence about the role of the brain area damaged than accidental lesions in humans.
- There are many similarities between brain structure and function in animals and humans so generalising from animal studies is useful.

lesioning

- Damage is caused to the brain (e.g. accidental in humans or surgery in animals).
- The animal is observed before and after lesioning.
- Looks for changes in behaviour that can be attributed to the damaged brain area.

weaknesses of lesioning

- Lesions are difficult to interpret because the behavioural changes may relate indirectly to the damage, e.g. feeding may stop due to pain or loss of sense of smell rather than a lack of motivation to eat.
- Case studies of brain damaged people rarely offer detailed pre-lesion behavioural information and cannot be replicated.
- Results from animals may not generalise to humans because our brains are not identical so will work in slightly different ways and additional factors (e.g. social or emotional ones) can affect human behaviour.

studying the brain

- Techniques can be either external such as CAT and EEG or invasive (physically entering the brain), e.g. lesioning.
- Information may be about structure and/or function of the brain.

strengths of EEG

- Non-invasive so avoids ethical problems of lesioning.
- Standard electrode placing ensures results are reliable.
- Participant is not affected by anaesthetics, radioactivity or being confined in a scanner so has higher validity than lesioning and scanning in some respects.

EEG (electroencephalogram)

- Records weak electrical activity from groups of active neurones using sensitive macroelectrodes on the head.
- Particular wave patterns are associated with specific brain activities such as different stages of sleep.

weaknesses of EEG

- Only measures average activity of many neurones, so results are crude indicators of brain function.
- The exact meaning of wave patterns and relation to brain function is unknown. They merely enable the researcher to differentiate brain states as they correlate with behaviour.

strengths of brain scanning

- Structural scans can identify brain abnormalities in living participants, which can be linked to psychological problems suggesting how brain areas affect behaviour.
- Structural scans can be used to measure brain volume which can be correlated to cognitive abilities and some are very detailed (e.g. MRI).
- A functional scan can be conducted while a participant performs an action (or doesn't), so is a more direct measure of the relationship between brain areas and associated behaviours or emotions than lesioning or structural scans of brain damage, e.g. Maguire et al. (1997) used PET scans to show that the hippocampus was active during recall of journeys by taxi drivers.

brain scanning

- CAT (computerised axial tomography): structural.
  - A series of x-rays is compiled by computer into a detailed image of structure.
  - Sequential scans can be made into a three-dimensional image.
- PET (positron emission tomography): functional.
  - Radioactive isotopes are injected into the blood and monitored to detect blood flow to active brain areas during different behaviours compared to baseline inactivity.
- MRI (magnetic resonance imaging): structural (MRI) or functional (fMRI).
  - Detects changes to a magnetic field caused by the brain.

weaknesses of brain scanning

- Scanners restrict movement so brain activity can only be studied in passive bodily states, e.g. listening or imagining.
- Exposure to scanning may need to be limited because of exposure to radioactivity.
- The scanner may be noisy and unfamiliar so affect participant's behaviour.

strengths of twin studies

- Twins provide a more valid comparison of shared genetic information than studies of siblings, as twins are the same age so are not subject to cohort effects.
- Twin studies have generated a large volume of data covering a wide variety of psychological variables.

twin studies

- Monozygotic (MZ) or identical twins share 100% of their genetic information.
- Dizygotic (DZ) or non-identical twins share, on average, 50% of their genes (and are no more genetically similar than siblings).
- If genes alone control a variable, MZ twins should be more similar than DZ twins.
- The percentage likelihood of both twins sharing a characteristic is called *concordance*.
- Higher concordance suggests a greater influence of genes.
- MZ twins reared together or separately can be compared.
- If genes alone control the variable, MZ twins should always be identical even when reared apart.
- If the environment is more important, MZ twins should be more similar when reared together than when reared apart.

weaknesses of twin studies

- MZ twins look alike and so are likely to be treated in exactly the same way by other people, creating a more similar environment for MZ twins than DZ twins.
- MZ twins may have more similar personalities so may make more similar choices than DZ twins, so their experiences are more similar.
- Separated twins may have had similar environments: with a relative, in the same village, at the same school. This makes it difficult to separate genetic and environmental effects.
- All MZ twins do not share the same uterine environment, which may be important in development but most twin studies fail to take this into account.
- As most people are not twins, the results from twin studies may not be representative or, therefore, generalisable.

studying the genetic influences on individual differences

- Correlational techniques look at the relationship between the appearance of two factors that may be linked.
- This method can be used to investigate the effect of genes compared to the environment on a psychological variable, such as schizophrenia, handedness, intelligence or personality.
- Genetic effects can be studied by comparing the similarity between individuals with differing relatedness (e.g. twin studies, family studies).
- Environmental effects can be investigated (or controlled for) in studies comparing shared or non-shared rearing environments.

strengths of adoption studies

- They directly compare the influence of genes versus the environment so have good face validity.
- Adoption studies have investigated a range of variables and used a variety of samples including comparisons of trans-racial adoptions, longitudinal studies and meta-analyses of the results of many other studies thereby obtaining a larger sample. The similarity of findings across techniques suggests good concurrent validity.

adoption studies

- Variables (such as personality or mental illness) are measured in parents and children, and are then correlated.
- A comparison is made between groups of adopted and non-adopted children.
- If adopted children resemble their natural parents, this supports the effect of genes. If they resemble their adoptive parents, this supports the effect of the environment.

weaknesses of adoption studies

- Rules for adoption now allow a wider range of individuals to adopt but, when many of the studies were conducted, adopting families all tended to be similar and middle class, potentially exaggerating apparent genetic influences.
- As most people are not adopted, samples of adoptees may not be representative so the results may not be generalisable.

strengths
of Dement & Kleitman

- The experiment was well-controlled because the participants did not drink alcohol or coffee during the day so their sleep would not have been affected by drug action.

- The reliability of judging REM and nREM sleep was high as the EEG is a scientific measure that is not affected by subjective judgements of the experimenters.

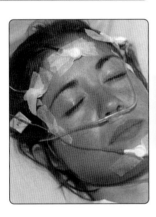

Dement & Kleitman (1957): eye movements and dreams study

Aim: to see whether dream content is related to eye movements during REM sleep.

Procedure: seven male and two female participants were asked not to consume alcohol or coffee during the daytime and spent the night in bed in a laboratory connected to an EEG. Eye movements were observed for distinctive patterns (mainly vertical, mainly horizontal, mixed, very few REMs). Participants were woken after 1 minute of regular REMs (and during nREM sleep) and asked to describe their dream content.

Findings: distinctive REM patterns were associated with dream content, e.g. a sleeper having vertical REMs was dreaming about climbing ladders and one with sudden horizontal eye movements to the left dreamt that a car had hit their vehicle from the left.

Conclusion: the pattern of REMs is strongly linked to dream content.

weaknesses
of Dement & Kleitman

- The sample was small and these individuals may not have been representative of the sleeping behaviour of everyone so the results may not be generalisable.

- The participants slept in a laboratory which was unfamiliar and had electrodes attached to their heads. This may have made it difficult for them to sleep normally so reducing the validity of the findings.

- If the participants were used to drinking alcohol or coffee, not doing so may have affected their sleep making it less typical.

strengths of Heston

- The control group was important because it showed that the increased incidence of schizophrenia in the adopted children of schizophrenic mothers was not the result of the adoption process itself as no controls developed schizophrenia.

- Similar findings from recent studies (e.g. Tienari et al., 1992) using more advanced techniques have confirmed the importance of genetics in schizophrenia.

Heston (1966): adoption study of schizophrenia

Aim: to investigate genetic influences on schizophrenia.

Procedure: 47 adults, adopted at birth because their mothers were schizophrenic were interviewed and compared to a control group of 47 adoptees whose mothers were not schizophrenic.

Findings: the interviews showed that five of the adults with schizophrenic mothers had been hospitalised with schizophrenic symptoms (10%). None of those whose mothers did not have schizophrenia had gone on to develop the disorder.

Conclusion: genes seem to play a role in schizophrenia as, even though they had not been brought up by their biological parents, children of the schizophrenic mothers were more likely to suffer from the disorder.

weaknesses of Heston

- As the mother's schizophrenia was the cause of adoption, they must have been severe cases. These results may not, therefore, generalise to people with milder schizophrenia.

- As the parent who was affected with schizophrenia was the mother, the children could have had environmental influences from the mother during gestation so the effect observed may not be entirely genetic.

- The study only measures the genetic influence from the mother on schizophrenia. This may not generalise to the effect of schizophrenia in fathers.

what different biological cycles exist?

- *Circadian rhythms:* daily cycles lasting 24 hours, such as the sleep/wake cycle.

- *Infradian rhythms:* cycles occurring less often than daily such as annual breeding cycles or the menstrual cycle.

- *Ultradian rhythms:* cycles occurring more often than daily, such as the 90-minute cycle of REM and nREM stages during sleep.

what are biological rhythms?

- Cycles that control bodily functions and behaviour.

- They are governed by both internal, bodily factors (endogenous) and external ones (zeitgebers).

- *Endogenous pacemakers* are physiological clocks that measure the passage of time relatively independently of external signals.

- *Zeitgebers* are cyclical external cues that provide a time base for biological rhythms.

how are circadian rhythms studied?

- The importance of the presence of zeitgebers can be determined by observing the change in length of circadian rhythms (of people and animals) in the absence of zeitgebers.

- Altering day length or the onset and offset of external cues (such as light) can be used to observe the effects on the circadian rhythms of people and animals.

- The effects of brain areas on circadian rhythms can be studied by lesioning.

- The effects of altered schedules of zeitgebers can be studied by observing the effects of flying across time zones and of changing shift.

how are circadian rhythms controlled?

- *Zeitgebers 'set' the biological clock* (a process called entrainment). If animals such as rats are kept in an artificial environment in which 12 hours of light are followed by 12 hours of darkness, but the exact timing of these periods is moved, the rats' activity cycle moves with the change (although not instantly). This shows that external cues regulate biological cycles. The light is detected by the retina and messages are sent to the *suprachiasmatic nucleus* (SCN).

- *Zeitgebers are not essential.* When rhythmical external signals are removed, cyclical behaviour continues (although the cycle length extends, e.g. to about 25 hours per day in humans). This shows that there is an internal or endogenous pacemaker. This is the role of the SCN, which sends signals to the *pineal gland*. These occur either when it is dark or at rhythmic intervals associated with dark phases. These signals instruct the pineal gland to secrete the hormone *melatonin*.

- *Zeitgebers keep the biological clock running to time.* If zeitgebers are absent (e.g. in continuous light or continuous darkness) biological clocks tend to 'free-run', that is the length of each 'daily' cycle extends. This shows that external factors regulate the internal clock.

evaluation of research into biological rhythms

- Studies on animals and people in controlled environments (such as sleep laboratories) allow researchers to be more certain that the factors they are manipulating, such as exposure to zeitgebers, are responsible for changes in rhythms. However, these studies may have lower ecological validity so their findings may not generalise to other, more realistic situations (such as airline staff). For example, Folkard (1996) studied a girl who was isolated for 25 days without daily cues to light. She was asked to play the bagpipes at what she believed to be the same time every day. Her playing became later as her day length extended. As she had no external cues, this showed that people's pacemakers free-run too. However, living in isolation is not representative of normal activity, e.g. she might have been bored and slept more.

- Lesioning studies, e.g. Ralph et al. (1990) show that the suprachiasmatic nucleus is involved in the control of sleep-wake cycles. They used two experimental groups of hamsters with either normal cycles or mutant cycles (which maintained a 20-hour rhythm). When they surgically removed cells from the SCN of one type of hamster and transferred it to the other, the recipient's cycle changed correspondingly.

- Much of the work on biological rhythms has been conducted on non-human animals whose rhythmical behaviour is different from our own, e.g. many are nocturnal or hibernate.

The SCN free-runs on a 25-hour cycle, so we find it easier to lengthen the day. This is called *phase delay* (we *delay* the time at which we reach any phase such as sleeping). We experience phase delay when we gain time (e.g. when the clocks go back or we fly east) or when shifts rotate with the clock so that, when changing shift pattern, we go to work later than we had previously. In either case, we go to bed later than we previously did, so the body clock can free-run.

reorganisational theory of dreams

- Dreams re-order memories.
- If sleep is disrupted, REM sleep will be limited.
- This may account for the confusion associated with jet lag and errors made by night shift workers.

restorational theory of sleep

- Sleep helps the body to recover from the day.
- If sleep is restricted, this is less effective.
- This could explain the tiredness and health problems arising from jet lag and shiftwork.

why is crossing time zones or changing shifts problematic?

Both jet lag and problems associated with shiftwork happen because the body's endogenous (internal) rhythm is set to a different cycle from the external demands (such as when we have to wake up or be attentive at work).

In both cases:

- This problem arises because the individual has to get up much earlier or go to bed much later than they used to *and carry on in this rhythm*.
- So their existing internal rhythm differs from the new cycle being imposed externally, that is, they are *desynchronised*.
- The necessary readjustment cannot occur instantly.

In *jet lag*, desynchronisation happens because time zones are crossed so the zeitgeber of the rising and setting of the sun occurs at times that differ from the endogenous rhythm.

In *shiftwork*, desynchronisation happens because employees must wake and sleep at times that differ from their previous cycle. Adjusting may be harder than with jet lag as, if they are moving to a night shift, the key zeitgeber of bright sunlight in the morning, which helps to entrain the new rhythm, will be absent.

The result is that we feel sleepy at the 'wrong' time of day but cannot sleep when we need to. Other aspects of our physiology (e.g. eating patterns) are also disrupted. The 'home' time zone rhythm, maintained by the SCN and its effect on melatonin from the pineal gland is at odds with the new 'day' and 'night'.

jet lag and shiftwork

- *Jet lag* is the syndrome of headaches, tiredness, etc. caused by losing (or to a lesser extent gaining) hours in a day by flying across time zones. This is especially dangerous for pilots.
- *Shiftwork* refers to a pattern of work that changes from daytime to working nights. This also can be dangerous, e.g. for healthcare workers.
- Taffinder et al. (1998) found that doctors deprived of sleep overnight made more errors on simulated operations.
- Both can cause irritability and illness (e.g. stomach upsets) and are linked to poor judgement, which may cause air crashes and industrial disasters, for example.
- Harma et al. (1994) found that flight attendants who crossed many time zones felt very sleepy and had cognitive deficits.

Sleep loss can arise in shift workers because:

- they want to socialise or use services in the daytime;
- bright daylight and noise may keep them awake;
- dim lighting at work on a night shift encourages them to feel sleepy when they need to be awake;
- shifts may change often, so re-synchronisation is never fully achieved.

overcoming desynchronisation

- Establishing a new rhythm takes time so each shift pattern should last at least three weeks.
- Readjustment is easier when the change results in phase delay so shifts should rotate forwards.
- Adjustment requires exposure to strong zeitgebers, e.g. daylight, so travellers should go outside and shift workers should have very bright lighting.
- Taking melatonin at bedtime can help to reset the body clock (Herxheimer & Petrie, 2001).

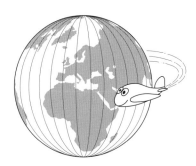

ecological theory of sleep

Sleep may have evolved to keep animals out of danger at times when they are poorly adapted. We, for instance, have poor vision at low light levels, so have evolved to sleep at night when it would be unsafe to move around. By sleeping, we keep ourselves still and quiet; thus, early in our evolutionary history, safe from nocturnal predators. Lucid dreaming could offer a mechanism to keep humans asleep – perhaps, unlike other mammals we 'get bored' more easily. The capacity to make dreams more interesting or pleasurable might have been advantageous because it kept early humans asleep for longer!

why is this a contemporary issue?

Current research is investigating the benefits derived from an ability to lucid dream and the practical ways in which it can be used (e.g. in therapy). Techniques for lucid dreaming are also increasingly being publicised, e.g. via the Internet. However, it is not yet clear whether there are risks attached to frequent and unsupervised use of the technique.

reorganisational theory of dreaming

This theory suggests that dreams allow the brain to sort memories out, removing unnecessary connections in the brain. Dreams arise as a by-product of this process. Lucid dreamers, in contrast to non-lucid dreamers, can alter the content of their dreams at will. By so doing, they must either:

- interrupt the 'sorting' process, which could result in ineffective reorganisation; or
- they may include their dream content into the reorganisational process.

Their memories should therefore be worse but there is no evidence for this.

activation-synthesis model of dreams

Lucid dreaming provides evidence to support the activation-synthesis model. Blagrove & Hartnell (2000) found a parallel in Locus of Control (the extent to which an individual perceives an internal responsibility for the events in their own life as opposed to luck or external forces) between waking and dreaming. Lucid dreamers tended to have a high locus of control when awake, suggesting that their cognitive style – the way they synthesise and interpret information – is similar during waking and dreaming.

lucid dreaming

This is a dream state in which the dreamer becomes aware that they are dreaming. This consciousness allows the lucid dreamer to:

- indicate to others that they are in a lucid dream;
- influence the content of their dream;
- wake themselves up at will.

physiological measurement

The existence of lucid dreaming overcomes one of the hurdles in sleep research – that the lowered state of consciousness of the sleeping participant prevents them from communicating with a researcher. Studies such as La Berge et al. (1981) have confirmed that the onset of the subjective experience of dreaming (which can be indicated by deliberate, pre-determined hand clenches or patterned eye movements) coincides with physiological measures of REM (recorded with an EOG) and the corresponding change in brain waves (detected with an EEG) – see the figure below.

lucid dreaming in therapy

Learning to control the course of dreams can help to reduce problems associated with disturbed sleep caused by nightmares (e.g. Brylowski, 1990). Other therapeutic uses have been suggested by Green & McCreery (1994), such as providing an outlet for sexual fulfilment for individuals who are unable to achieve this in waking life due to physical disability or problems with their gender identity.

restorational theory of sleep

Sleep, according to this theory, serves as a minimum-output time during which the body can direct its reserves of energy towards growth and repair, rather than daily activities such as thinking and moving. Since the brain is the body's largest consumer of energy, lucid dreaming ought not to exist, as it appears to place unnecessary demands on body systems. At the least, lucid dreaming should result in tiredness but Green & McCreery report that lucid dreamers awaken feeling well rested and positive, contradicting the predictions of resorational theory.

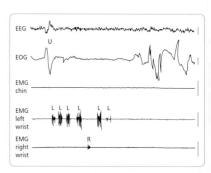

A participant's up-down eye movement and series of hand clenches signal lucid dreaming.

theories

- Describe the relationship between EEG criteria and sleep stages.
- Define the terms 'exogenous pacemaker' and 'zeitgeber'.
- Describe how these two mechanisms control circadian rhythms.
- Outline **one** physiological explanation for why we dream.
- Describe **two** criticisms of this theory of dreaming.

general assumptions

One general assumption from the physiological approach is the importance of the nervous system.

- Using any example described here, or another example of your choice, outline ways in which the nervous system is important in the control of behaviour.

studies

- Identify **two** studies from the physiological approach.
- Describe either **two** similarities or **two** differences in the procedures of these experiments and explain why you think these differences may be important.

St Monica's is a teaching hospital that has a wing for sleep problems. Research teams based there investigate both normal and atypical sleep patterns.

Sean, a medical student, has just started on night shifts. He is finding it hard to sleep in the daytime, even though he is in hospital accommodation with other night shift workers – so it is dark and quiet when he is trying to sleep.

application

- Define the term 'circadian rhythm'.
- Explain why Sean is having difficulty sleeping even though it is dark and quiet.
- Outline some other problems that Sean might experience as a result of his shiftwork.
- Explain **two** strategies the hospital could implement to make night shifts easier.

research methods

- The hospital where Sean works has a sleep laboratory and a group of Sean's peers decide to conduct some research into the effects of night shifts on sleep.
  - What technique could they use to monitor time spent asleep and different sleep stages of participants?
  - Describe **two** strengths and **two** weaknesses of this technique.
- One participant they test hardly appears to be dreaming at all. She suggests it is because she received a gunshot wound to her head when she was very small. Until then she remembered lots of dreams, but they stopped very suddenly as a result of the accident.
  - Outline **one** technique that could be used to investigate her brain structure to look for the location of any damage.
  - Describe **two** advantages and **two** disadvantages of this technique.
- What methods of investigating the brain are illustrated below?

contemporary issue

A participant called John volunteers for the research that Sean and his friends are conducting in the sleep lab. When Sean interviews John after his first sleep lab session, John describes a dream in which he 'chose' what would happen next. He seems surprised, then rather worried, when Sean tells him that this is unusual and called lucid dreaming.

- Use your knowledge of the physiological approach to describe the phenomenon of lucid dreaming.
- Consider the extent to which John's fears are well founded. Is it likely that lucid dreaming is harmful or beneficial?

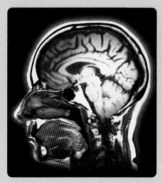 

This rat was given surgery that damaged a brain region called the ventromedial hypothalamus (VMH) that controls motivation to eat. As a consequence, it eats to excess.

theories

- Outline the events in a typical night's sleep. You may use diagrams in your answer (but diagrams alone are not sufficient).
- Outline **one** theory of sleep.
- Describe **two** strengths and **two** weaknesses of the theory you have outlined.
- Compare and contrast this theory to any other theory of sleep.

general assumptions

One general assumption from the physiological approach is the influence of genetics on behaviour.

- Using any example described here, or another example of your choice, outline ways in which genes influence behaviour.

studies

- Describe **one** study from the physiological approach.
- Evaluate the study you have identified in terms of **two** strengths and two weaknesses.

Ali and Mo are identical twins whose parents volunteered, when the twins were born, to be part of a longitudinal study. The twins are now 23 years old. Mo's job requires him to fly occasionally from London to New York.

contemporary issue

Hypnosis, like sleeping and dreaming, appears to be an altered state of awareness. It can be induced in some, but not all, people by a hypnotist. A hypnotised person is less responsive to their environment but can hear and respond to suggestions from the hypnotist.

Use your knowledge of the physiological approach to answer the following questions.

- Describe **two** methods that could be used to investigate whether hypnosis is an altered state of consciousness and explain what you would expect to find if hypnotised people were in a different state of awareness.
- It is possible that susceptibility to hypnosis is genetically controlled. Suggest how you might investigate whether this is the case.

research methods

- In the most recent session in the twin study, Mo and Ali were tested for various personality measures. The results from a group of monozygotic twins (like Mo and Ali) were compared to those of a group of dizygotic (non-identical) twins.

  - What technique would be used to analyse the similarity between twins?

  - If the results of twins such as Mo and Ali were more similar than those of non-identical twins, what conclusion would you draw about the cause of such characteristics?

  - How could this conclusion be criticised?

  - Outline **one** technique that could be used as an alternative to twin studies in this situation.

- Mo and Ali have had brain scans every two years to find out whether their brains are developing at the same rate.

  - Identify **one** technique that could be used for this.

  - Describe **one** advantage and one disadvantage of this type of brain scan.

- What method of investigating the brain is illustrated opposite?

application

- What problems might Mo experience as a consequence of the travelling he does?
- Use evidence from the physiological approach to explain why these problems arise.
- Identify **two** pieces of evidence you have used above and evaluate them.

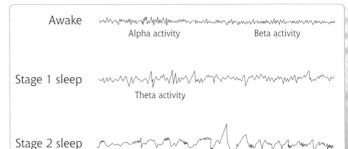

chapter 7
revision

making it work 80

making the best of your time 81

making revision worthwhile 82

making ideas stick 83

improving your exam technique 84

unit 1 revision checklist 85

unit 2 revision checklist 87

making it work

how to get started

You know there's a lot to learn, but it's often difficult to motivate yourself to work because you sort of 'know it all already'. The ideas are all familiar, but you have to make sure that your knowledge is sufficiently sound to answer any question that crops up in an exam. So, what can you do?

The ideas on this page are designed to help you to understand how and why you need to revise. Over the following four pages, you can explore some of these ideas in detail to help you to plan and conduct your revision effectively.

what can you do to make the ideas stick?

- Repetition
- Deep processing
- Application

what can you do to make revision worthwhile?

- Know what it is you are supposed to understand
- Know how you are going to be tested

how can you improve your exam technique?

- Practise answering questions – use the ones at the end of each chapter to help you.
- Answer the exam-style questions in Chapter 8 before looking at the worked examples and guidance – you can learn from any mistakes you make.
- Pace yourself – make sure that you note the time when you start answering a paper. In the final exams you have 90 minutes to answer 72 marks worth of questions – that's only just over a minute per mark.

how can you keep yourself motivated?

- Set achievable goals.
- Keep working once you've started so that you achieve a target, but then give yourself a break.
- Entertain yourself with coloured pens and paper, and music if you can concentrate.
- Work with a friend or get someone to read you questions or answer them aloud to your dog/teddy bear/parent.

is time on your side?

- Start revising early – the AS Psychology exams are often before the summer half-term holiday and you may not have had much, or any, study leave before the exam date.
- Organise your revision – allow yourself enough time to revise both units. There's no point in being great at Unit 1 if you know nothing about Unit 2. Write yourself a revision plan.
- Make sure that you are using your days effectively – if you aren't sure, try the 'time circles' on the next page.

where should you direct your effort?

- Be sure that you know the marks each paper carries – Units 1 and 2 are equally weighted, so they are both important.
- Make yourself aware of your strong and weaker areas. Look through the introduction pages at the start of each chapter (*what you need to know*).
- Use the 'traffic light' method – identify what you are certain that you understand (label it in green), the areas that you are fairly confident about (label these in orange) and use red for any aspects that you feel less happy with. You must still revise the green and orange sections, but make sure that you pay special attention to the red and leave yourself enough time to seek help if you need to.

your revision plan

- Think of each exam as a deadline – what do you have to achieve before that deadline?
- Break up the work in to equivalent sections in terms of marks or how much work you know you have to do to remember them (think about the 'traffic light' system).
- Spread the sections out over the available time so that you know how quickly you have to get through each part.
- If you know that you are likely to 'get behind', plan in some 'spare' time to catch up.
- Bear in mind that the amount of time you can spend each day will depend on other commitments – be realistic.

Make a plan like this and try to stick to it.

approach	target start date	target end date
social		
cognitive		
cognitive-developmental		
physiological		
psychodynamic		
learning		
exam date		

daily timetable

- Try to organise yourself so that there are fixed hours on all or most of the days of the week that you set aside for revision.
- It is much better to spread out your learning than to cram it in at the end.
- Write out a timetable to remind yourself that you need to be working.
- You will find it much easier to keep to this if other aspects of your work are organised too. Try to have a work space in the house – a corner of your room perhaps, but not where there are distractions like a television or where other people can disturb you.

This timetable isn't likely to suit you exactly, but try to write one that starts you working early in the day and includes breaks. Write in some leisure time too.

	Mon	Tues	Wed	Thur	Fri	Sat	Sun
9–10							
10–11							
break							
11.15–12.15							
12.15–1.15							
lunch							
2.15–3.15							
break							
3.30–4.30							
break							
6–7							
7–8							

time circles: how good are you at sticking to your intended plan?

If you don't think that you are making good use of your day, stop and fill out these time circles ... but remember ... this isn't a substitute for work!
If you counted up the hours you have spent on each activity, what would your current and ideal time circles look like? Do you have your priorities right?

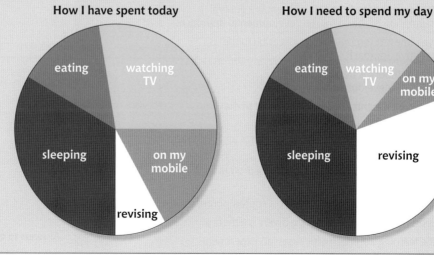

How I have spent today

How I need to spend my day

know what you are supposed to understand

On the Unit 1 and Unit 2 exams some of the things you need to understand are determined for you by the specification. Other aspects offer choices.

- You can be tested on any of the particular examples of general assumptions, studies, theories, research methods and applications that are dictated by the specification.

- In addition, you can be asked for examples of general assumptions, studies, theories and contemporary issues that you have learned about.

- Each chapter of this book starts with a page telling you those things that you must know and possible examples of choices – use these to guide you.

- There are also two checklists at the end of this chapter to help you to summarise the things you need to learn.

know how you are going to be tested

- Make sure that you have seen a whole exam paper. They follow typical formats and you don't want to be shocked.

- Know what kinds of questions are generally asked. (The questions throughout this book will give you a good idea.)

- Be aware of the different terms that are used in exam questions and what they mean (these are specifically *not* published by the exam board because they could change or include different ones, so don't be surprised if some questions are unfamiliar). There is a list of typical terms at the end of this chapter.

- Don't be fooled into expectations about exam papers – they can change. For example:

  - The last question on Units 1 and 2 is generally an essay. It doesn't have to be.

  - It is often on applications or contemporary issues, but again it doesn't have to be.

  - Contemporary issue questions often ask for 'a contemporary issue that you have studied', they don't have to – a question could present you with an unfamiliar contemporary issue to analyse.

  - Alternative essay-style questions could be about describing and evaluating theories, studies or research methods or linking detailed areas of study to general assumptions.

try this quick quiz

statement	true or false
1 The information processing approach is a theory.	
2 Piaget's stages are a theory.	
3 Analysis of symbols is a general assumption.	
4 The three mountains study is from the cognitive approach.	
5 EEGs are a research method from the psychodynamic approach.	
6 The importance of genetics is a general assumption from the physiological approach.	
7 Social identity theory is an explanation for prejudice.	
8 The importance of early experience is a general assumption from the psychodynamic approach.	
9 Operant conditioning is a theory.	
10 Milgram studied obedience.	
11 The importance of the environment is a general assumption of the cognitive-developmental approach.	
12 Eyewitness testimony is an application in the cognitive approach.	
13 Agency theory is from the cognitive-developmental approach.	
14 Field experiments are commonly used in the social approach.	
15 Deliberately altering human behaviour is an application from the learning approach.	
16 Longitudinal studies are a research method from the cognitive approach.	
17 Freud's ideas about dreaming are a contemporary issue.	
18 Godden & Baddeley's work on divers is a theory.	
19 The learning approach often uses lab experiments.	

Answers to quick quiz:
1E 2T 3F 4F 5F 6T 7T 8T 9T 10T 11F 12T 13F 14T 15T 16F 17F 18F 19T

how can you make information sink in?

repetition

If you studied the multistore model, you will know that recall relies on consolidation of material into long-term memory by repeating it so that it is transferred from short-term memory. This means you need to go over material several times, for example:

- writing summary notes;
- reading them over;
- answering questions.

deep processing

- If you studied the levels of processing theory you will know that recall is better when information is encoded through semantic processing. This means that you have to think about the material you are learning – just copying it out isn't enough.
- Explaining the ideas on paper, or to other people, helps with this.
- Set up a telephone network between yourself and your friends so that you ask and answer each other's questions.

application

- Use what you know as often as you can. Try to think about how you can explain the behaviour of people around you, in books or on the TV, using the ideas you have learned.
- Try the questions in the box opposite to give you an idea of ways to use what you know.

psychology in the real world – making yourself think!

- You go to parties on both Friday night and Saturday night. On Friday you stay up till 2 a.m., on Saturday till 4 a.m. On Sunday it's really hard to go to sleep at your 'normal' weekday time. Why?

- In the book you are reading, there is a character who has an eating disorder. The story alternates between his adult life and his childhood. In the chapters about the early years, his mother disappears when he is 10 months old and he has to move from home to home as his father searches for work. What would Freud say was the cause of the eating disorder?

- Your mum goes upstairs to get a jumper. She stops to say hello to you in your room, then can't remember why she went upstairs so goes back down without the jumper. As soon as she's back downstairs she remembers. Why?

- Your 4-year-old cousin is watching the TV. She cries when they shut the teddy bears in the cupboard at the end of the show. She wails that they will be frightened in the dark. Why?

- The newspaper you are reading has an interview column. The interviewee, who had a lousy time at boarding school, says that making you do pointless tasks at school just because you are told to is good preparation for adult life. He claims that you need to be able to accept that the institution comes first. How could you explain this view?

- A magazine problem page you are reading described how a couple were badly burned whilst having sex in a tent. When asked why they were burning candles rather than using their torch, they said they could only reach orgasm with the smell of candles, so torchlight wouldn't work. How could this happen and what could the agony aunt advise?

- People are complaining that children's heroes on TV shouldn't swear so much because it is encouraging their sons and daughters to copy them. Are they justified in this fear?

- At a friend's house, his mum is giving his younger brothers lunch. Each has had a whole can of cola emptied into a glass, but the glasses are different shapes. The boys are arguing about who has the most. Why don't they understand that they both have the same amount?

terms that are often used in exam questions – what do they mean?

injunction	definition	A01 and/or A02?
apply	explain a phenomenon in the real world, e.g. using concepts and theories	
assess	judge the value of something, such as a theory or study, by looking at its strengths and weaknesses	
compare	look for similarities between things, e.g. two research methods or two theories	
contrast	look for differences between two things	
define	state the meaning of a term	
describe	present details, e.g. of a general assumption or key application, without explaining it	
discuss	describe a phenomenon and comment on it, e.g. by evaluation or application	
distinguish	identify the features that make two things different, e.g. two research methods or two theories	
evaluate	judge the value of something, such as a theory or study, by looking at its strengths and weaknesses perhaps in contrast to an alternative	
explain	give a clear account of a topic	
identify	make a particular example recognisable, e.g. one study or theory	
name	identify an example, e.g. of a study or theory, by giving its title or the author(s)	
outline	briefly describe the main points, e.g. of a theory or contemporary issue, without explaining it	
state	indicate a clear awareness of a particular point	

Remember – these are not the only words that can be used. You may have to 'think on your feet'

what are these questions asking you to do?

- **Explain** how circadian rhythms are controlled.
- **Name** one defence mechanism.
- **State** two causes of forgetting.
- **Outline** one strength of agency theory.
- **Describe** one study from the physiological approach.
- **Evaluate** Milgram's research into obedience.
- **Compare** two theories of memory.
- **Contrast** Piaget's theory with one other theory of cognitive development.
- **Define** the terms 'positive reinforcement' and 'negative reinforcement'.
- **Discuss** a contemporary issue from the psychodynamic approach.
- **Apply** the social identity theory to the following situation:
  A TV report says that tension is rising between pro- and anti-hunt groups and they are becoming increasingly violent.
- **Identify** one general assumption from the learning approach.
- **Assess** the usefulness of theories of cognitive development in education.
- **Distinguish** between the conscious and the unconscious mind.

You will need to be able to:

social approach

Describe **two** general assumptions of the social approach:
(*e.g. influence of individuals, groups, society and culture*)

Describe and evaluate **two** theories of prejudice:
(SIT and **one other**, e.g. *discursive theory*)

social identity theory

Describe and evaluate **two** theories of obedience:
(agency theory and **one other**, e.g. *charismatic leadership*)

agency theory

Describe and evaluate **two** studies from the social approach:
(**Milgram** and **one other**, e.g. *Hofling et al.*)

Milgram's theory of obedience

Describe and evaluate the **two** research methods commonly
used in the social approach:

field experiments

surveys

Discuss the application for the social approach:

reduction of prejudice

Discuss a contemporary issue from the social approach:
(e.g. *social life on the Internet*)

cognitive approach

Describe **two** general assumptions of the cognitive approach:

information processing

computer analogy

Describe and evaluate **two** theories of memory:
(e.g. *multistore model* and *levels of processing*)

Describe and evaluate **two** theories of forgetting:
(e.g. *displacement* and *cue dependent forgetting*)

Describe and evaluate **two** studies from the
cognitive approach:
(e.g. *Craik & Tulving* and *Aggleton & Waskett*)

continued

Describe and evaluate the **two** research methods commonly used in the cognitive approach:

experiments

case studies of brain damaged people

Discuss the **application** for the cognitive approach:

eyewitness testimony

Discuss a **contemporary issue** from the cognitive approach: (e.g. *flashbulb memories*)

cognitive-developmental approach

Describe **two** general assumptions from the cognitive-developmental approach:

importance of cognitive abilities

development of cognitive abilities over time

Describe and evaluate **Piaget's stage theory**:

Piaget's stage theory

Describe and evaluate **Piaget's research**:

Piaget's research

Describe and evaluate **one other** theory of cognitive-development: (e.g. *Vygotsky*)

Describe and evaluate **two** studies from the cognitive-developmental approach:
(e.g. *Baillargeon & De Vos. This could include some of Piaget's research.*)

Describe and evaluate **two** research methods commonly used in the cognitive-developmental approach:

longtitudinal studies

observations

Discuss the **application** for the cognitive-developmental approach:

education

Discuss a **contemporary issue** from the cognitive-developmental approach: (e.g. *computers in education*)

learning approach

Describe **two** general assumptions of the learning approach:

importance of the environment

processes of learning

Describe **three** theories of learning and evaluate them as explanations for human learning:

classical conditioning

operant conditioning

social learning theory

Describe and evaluate **two** studies from the learning approach: (e.g. *Watson & Raynor* and *Skinner – superstitious pigeons*)

Describe and evaluate the **two** research methods commonly used in the learning approach:

animal learning studies

laboratory experiments

Discuss the application for the learning approach:

deliberately changing people's behaviour

Discuss a contemporary issue from the learning approach: (e.g. *media violence*)

psychodynamic approach

Describe **two** general assumptions of the pschodynamic approach:

importance of unconscious mind and motivation

importance of early experience

Describe and evaluate Freud's theory of the unconscious and psychosexual development:

Freud's model of the mind

Freud's theory of psychosexual development

Freud's concept of defence mechanisms

Describe and evaluate Freud's theory of dreaming:

Freud's theory of dreaming

Describe and evaluate **one other** psychodynamic theory: (e.g. *Erikson*)

Describe and evaluate **two** studies from the psychodynamic approach: (e.g. *Adams* and *Freud – Little Hans*)

continued

Describe and evaluate the **three** research methods commonly used in the psychodynamic approach:

> *case studies of people in therapy*

> *analysis of symbols*

> *clinical interviews*

Discuss the application for the psychodynamic approach:

> *mental health*

Discuss a contemporary issue from the psychodynamic approach: (e.g. *Buffy*)

>

physiological approach

Describe **two** general assumptions of the physiological approach:

> *importance of genetics*

> *importance of the nervous system*

Describe and evaluate **two** theories of sleep: (restorational and **one other**, e.g. *ecological theory*)

> *restorational theory of sleep*

>

Describe and evaluate **one** physiological theory of dreaming: (e.g. *activation synthesis*)

>

Describe the patterns of sleep and dreaming, and the control of circadian rhythms:

> *circadian rhythms, cycles of sleep and dreams*

Describe and evaluate **two** studies from the physiological approach: (e.g. *Dement & Kleitman* and *Heston*)

>

Describe and evaluate research methods commonly used in the physiological approach:

> *brain scans*   *lesioning*
> *EEG*   *correlations*

Discuss the application for the physiological approach:

> *jet lag and shiftwork*

Discuss a contemporary issue from the physiological approach: (e.g. *lucid dreaming*)

>

chapter 8
examination questions

worked examples: unit 1   90

worked examples: unit 2   93

assessment objectives revisited 96

The style of questions in the papers for Unit 1 and Unit 2 is the same so, although this chapter is divided into two parts, this is simply so that you can practise questions according to the topics that you have been revising. Across the questions discussed for the two unit examinations, a range of possible styles is covered. These are not the only ones – exams may include new types of questions from time to time – but they do illustrate a variety, and the strategies you will need to answer all questions well.

There are several ways that you could use this chapter. Here are some suggestions:

● reading it through, carefully comparing the student's responses and the commentary provided so that you understand where marks were gained and missed;

● working with a partner, one person could read out the question and answer, while the second person comments on whether they believe the answer is correct – say how many marks you would give it and why. Both of you can then discuss the commentary;

● with a few exceptions (like the first question below) you could work through the questions alone, covering up each answer, writing a response to the question yourself, and reviewing your answer using the guidance in the commentary.

Please note that the questions used are from Edexcel examination papers but the answers are the author's, and Edexcel is not responsible for their accuracy.

worked examples: unit 1

Question 1

The three statements below all relate to longitudinal studies. For each statement write in the box next to it whether it is a strength or a weakness of the longitudinal research method.

Statement	Strength or weakness
As the participants live in their natural environment during the course of the study, they will be affected by variables other than the ones being studied.	strength ✗
Because of the time involved, many participants may drop out.	weakness ✔
The same participants can be tested repeatedly over the duration of the study.	strength ✔

[3]
(January 2005)

It is common for unit papers to start with an 'easy' question, often one requiring a task such as matching boxes or ticking and crossing. This question looks superficially simple, but the very first part could catch you out if you don't read the statement carefully. The first phrase – about participants living in their natural environment – sounds like it could be a strength, but the end of the statement – saying that they will be affected by other variables – makes it clear that in this instance it is a disadvantage. The candidate falls into this trap so misses a mark. It is worth noting that if you wrote more than one word in a box it would be marked as incorrect.

Question 2

Outline the computer analogy as it is used in cognitive psychology.

This says that brains work like computers, ✔ *taking information in (through senses like a computer does through the keyboard or mouse) and processing it.* ✔ *Thinking about this similarity can help psychologists to understand how human brains might deal with information, store it and retrieve it.* ✔

[3]
(January 2005)

This question is asking you to briefly describe a named general assumption. You do not need to evaluate it or apply it, although an example of how it can be applied may help you to make your description clear.

The first sentence of the answer given is brief but is just enough to gain the mark for identifying the assumption. This could alternatively have been gained by observing the comparison that both have input/processing/output, but these points would not *both* have gained marks. The example earns a second mark, and other examples could have been given for a further mark. The final mark is for describing the function of the analogy – to understand how minds work. Note that if this had been purely evaluative (such as computers are more complex so don't help us to understand human minds), this mark would not have been given.

Question 3

(a) Outline **one** general assumption of the social approach.

Being a member of a group affects our behaviour. ✔ *We tend to be biased towards members of our own group, favouring them over non-members,* ✔ *this is called in-group/out-group.*   **[3]**

This differs from the previous example of a question about a general assumption because here you can choose which to describe.

The candidate has made a suitable choice but has missed the third mark – their final point effectively restates what they have already described. The easiest way to earn this last mark would have been to explain an example, such as stereotyped beliefs about a different ethnic group.

(b) Name **two** studies from the social approach.

First study   *Milgram* ✗

Second study   *Hofling's study with the nurses* ✔   **[2]**

If you are asked to identify a study, the easiest way to do it is by stating the researcher(s) name(s). However, if they have conducted many similar studies, you also need the date to make it clear which study you mean – hence why the candidate has not earned a mark for 'Milgram'. You can alternatively give a 'title' for the study – think about how you could look the study up in a book.

(c) Outline a strength and a weakness of **one** of the studies you have named in (b).

Strength   *Milgram's shock study was good because the participants didn't know that they were being tested for obedience so behaved normally even though it was an experimental setting* ✔ *and this helped us to understand why people are obedient in real life.* ✔   **[2]**

Weakness   *People wouldn't normally expect to give electric shocks to other people so the study lacked validity.* ✔ *This matters because it means that the findings might not apply to many real world situations.* ✔   **[2]**

(January 2004)

Question 4

(a) Explain what is meant by the following terms in relation to Social Identity Theory.

Social categorisation   *Dividing people, including ourselves, into members of different groups* ✔ *according to their characteristics*   **[2]**

Social identification   *Indicating that we belong to a group by adopting its identity* ✔ *and behaving in a way that fits this group identity* ✔   **[2]**

Social comparison   *Judging how good your own group is in relation to others.* ✔ *It is important that we judge our group to be better because this preserves self esteem.* ✔   **[2]**

The answer to the first part of this question began well but the second mark was missed because the idea was not explained sufficiently. The candidate could have gone on to say, for example, '... based on stereotyped judgements about their appearance'.

Note that, although it is generally better to avoid using the word that you are defining in your definition (such as saying obedience is obeying others), it is almost impossible in the second part. Referring to the idea of 'belonging' makes this a good answer.

The third part again answered well, although it was quite long for 2 marks.

Even though these two points contradict one another, they are both appropriate evaluations of Milgram's study. Note that the two points must refer to the same study and that, even though the student wasn't awarded the mark for 'Milgram' in part (b), it was obvious what they were talking about in (c) so it was still possible for them to earn marks.

(b) Give **one** strength and **one** weakness of using
   Social Identity Theory as an explanation of prejudice.

Strength   *One strength is that is supported*
by evidence such as Tajfel (1970). ✔   [2]

This is not sufficient for both marks. The candidate needed
to go on to say *how* Tajfel's evidence supports SIT, for example
by observing that it shows the prejudiced feelings arise
as a result of *comparisons*.

Weakness   *It doesn't explain why there are*
individual differences in prejudice, ✔ *some people*
are more prejudiced than others and SIT cannot
account for this.   [2]

Again, this is not sufficient for both marks. Even though
the answer appears to have two ideas, the second phrase
is actually the same point as the first expressed differently –
either would have earned the mark. The candidate needed
to continue and say, for instance, that such observations
can be explained by personality differences.

(c) Outline **two** strategies to reduce prejudice.

First strategy   *Inter-group contact* ✔ *is where*
people from different groups are forced to encounter
each other, ✔ *such as described by Deutsch & Collins*
(1951) who compared white and black Americans
in racially mixed areas and racially segregated
areas – the people in the mixed areas were less
prejudiced. ✔ *This kind of contact helps people to*
see that their stereotypes are wrong which reduces
social categorisation and so reduces prejudice.   [3]

Second strategy   *Co-operation is another way*
to reduce prejudice. ✔ *Co-operation is where people*
from conflicting groups are given a shared goal. ✔
This aims to limit identification because they need
to rely on each other in order to achieve the aim
which means that they are more likely to find
reasons to value members of the other group. ✔   [3]

(January 2004)

The answer for the first strategy uses evidence to illustrate
the answer. This is one way to elaborate the answer. The last
sentence would also have gained a mark but 3 marks had
already been awarded. The second strategy earns marks
by elaborating the description of the technique.

Question 5

(a) Outline **one** contemporary issue you have studied
from the Cognitive Approach.

Flashbulb memories are a contemporary issue ✔
because they seem to be more vivid and accurate
than most long term memories ✔ *but research*
suggests that they may not be as special as people
have claimed. They are supposed to be different
because they are the result of emotional situations
such as traumatic events like 9-11. ✔   [3]

This answer indicates both what the issue is and why it is a
contemporary issue – because there is debate about the
nature of these memories, i.e. whether they are special or not.

(b) Use **one or more** concepts from the Cognitive
   Approach to explain the issue you have outlined in (a).

In general, long-term memories (LTM) fade and we
only retain the gist of events, but flashbulb memories
seem to be different. This might be because flashbulb
memories are more emotional than other LTM.
Davidson & Glisky (2002) found recall of Princess
Diana's death was better than recall of Mother
Theresa's death which happened at the same time
but was a less emotionally arousing event. ✔
This supports the idea that flashbulb memories are
special because it might be important to remember
dangerous events well as this could enhance
survival. ✔ *But this isn't good evidence because*
there would have been much more publicity of
Princess Diana's death so the difference might just
be because of more rehearsal. ✔ *Other evidence also*
supports the idea – such as Bohannon & Symons
(1992) who showed that recall of the Challenger
space shuttle disaster was better in people who were
more upset. ✔

Cue dependent theory suggests that flashbulb
memories aren't special because all the information
encoded at the time of the event could act as state
and context cues to help retrieve the memories. ✔
Levels of processing theory would say that because we

continued on next page

continued from previous page

have flashbulb memories for socially important events, we would process the information at a semantic level as we tried to understand why they happened – like 9-11. This deep processing would therefore be the cause of recall rather than anything special about flashbulb memories. ✔

[6]

(January 2005)

The first two sentences are superfluous – they restate the answer in part (a). However, the remaining content is all relevant. There is a good balance between evidence 'for' and evidence 'against' the idea. Although this is less important here, it would matter in a longer (essay-style) answer that was being marked for 'balance' as well as for content. AO2 marks are being gained in three different ways: for relating the issue to theories (such as rehearsal or cue dependency), for evaluating the idea using evidence (such as Davidson & Glisky, 2002), and for considering the worth of this evidence in relation to the issue.

worked examples: unit 2

Question 1

Place a tick (✔) in the boxes next to the **three** statements that are correct.

Statement	Tick or leave blank	
Dreams are more likely in REM sleep.	✓	✔
The body is not paralysed in REM sleep.	✓	✗
Dreams are less likely in REM sleep.		
Brain activity increases during REM sleep.	✓	✔
Eye movements do not occur in REM sleep.		
The body is paralysed in REM sleep.		

[3]

(January 2005)

Although this was not the first question on this particular paper, it is a common format for the opening question. You will need to beware of questions like this. They look simple but it is easy to get caught out if you don't read every statement carefully. The candidate has made a mistake and missed an easy mark because they have misread the second line, which says 'The body is *not* paralysed in REM sleep', expecting it to read as the last line (the correct answer) does.

It is worth noting that if you tick more than the required three boxes, your whole table would be marked as incorrect.

Question 2

In a classical conditioning experiment, a dog was conditioned to salivate to a bell by repeatedly pairing the food and the sound of the bell. The conditioned response of salivation became associated with the conditioned stimulus of the bell ringing.

(a) (i) After conditioning, the bell was rung many times without food being presented. What happened to the conditioned response?

Eventually the dog won't salivate at the sound of the bell. ✔ *This is called extinction.* ✔ [2]

(ii) Several weeks later, the bell was rung again and the dog salivated. What is this process called?

Spontaneous recovery ✔ [1]

The answer for part (a) (i) gives an explanation and the term. Alternatively, the candidate could have gained full marks for a more detailed explanation without the term, as the term itself is not specifically asked for.

(b) In the past, studies in the learning approach often used animals. Outline **two** strengths and **two** weaknesses of using animals to study learning.

Strength 1 *Some animals are similar to humans, such as other mammals, particularly primates, so are good models for human behaviour* ✔ *because they have a similar nervous system and learn in similar ways.* ✔ [2]

continued on next page

continued from previous page

Strength 2   *Animals can be used in experiments where the controls would cause distress to human participants.* ✔   **[2]**

Strength 1 is good but strength 2 is not sufficient for both marks. The candidate needed to go on to say *how* this was possible – for example because the guidelines for animals allow greater control over an animal's environment – or *why* this matters – so experiments on animals can explore issues that cannot be studied on humans such as isolation or deprivation.

Weakness 1   *Findings from studies on animals may not generalise to humans* ✔ *because we have bigger brains and can learn in different ways from animals.* ✔   **[2]**

Weakness 2   *Because more controlled environments can be imposed on animals, they may suffer more than people, which is unethical.* ✔   **[2]**

(January 2004)

Weakness 1 is good but weakness 2 is not sufficient for both marks. The candidate needed to continue and for instance say that this matters in studies using animals because the findings may not be valid if the animal is in distress.

Question 3

The deliberate alteration of human behaviour is an application of the learning approach.

(a) Describe **one** way in which human behaviour has been deliberately altered by psychologists using operant conditioning.

A token economy is where people get positive reinforcements in the form of tokens (such as punches in a card) each time they perform a behaviour that is desired by the institution ✔ *such as getting patients in mental institutions to wash and get dressed.* ✔ *The tokens are only secondary reinforcers* ✔ *so when there are enough marks on their card this can be swapped for a treat,*

e.g. sweets, this is the primary reinforcer. ✔ *This works because the tokens are associated with the primary reinforcers through classical conditioning* ✔ *and the reinforcement results in the good behaviours such as washing being performed more often.*   **[5]**

(January 2004)

This is a good answer. Note that the reference to classical conditioning earns a mark here because it is explaining how the token economy (a system based on operant conditioning) works. An answer that related only to a technique based on classical conditioning – such as aversion therapy – would not gain marks. The final phrase does not receive a mark only because the candidate has already reached the maximum, it would have done otherwise.

Question 4

(a) Freud's theory of dreaming makes a distinction between manifest content and latent content.

What did Freud mean by **manifest content**?

The storyline of the dream that we can remember ✔ *that contains symbols representing the latent content.* ✔   **[2]**

What did Freud mean by **latent content**?

The underlying meaning of the dream ✔ *such as hidden guilt about sex.* ✔   **[2]**

The first part gains full marks for a detailed explanation, the second part gains the second mark for an example. Alternatively this mark could have been earned by further explanation, such as saying 'this protects us from repressed fears'.

These should be easy marks but the two terms are often muddled up. If the answers had been reversed, the candidate would have gained no marks at all. In situations like this it is worth learning a mnemonic to help you.

(b) Name **two** defence mechanisms.

1   *Repression* ✔

2   *Reaction formation* ✔   **[2]**

(c) According to Freud, why do we use defence
   mechanisms?

Defence mechanisms hide thoughts from
consciousness so protect us from being aware
of painful or guilty thoughts ✔ *because they change*
the real fear or guilt and express it differently. ✔
For example in reaction formation a person who is
frightened because they think they are gay might
be homophobic and hide their true feelings. ✔   **[3]**

The answer above explains the function of defence mechanisms
in general, then gives an example. Marks could alternatively
have been gained by looking at one mechanism in detail.

(d) Evaluate Freud's explanation of defence mechanisms.

Evidence like Adams shows that defence mechanisms,
such as reaction formation, exist because the
homophobic men were more aroused by the gay porn
suggesting that they had unconscious homosexual
desires. ✔ *This is good evidence because it was from*
a well-controlled laboratory experiment, whereas
a lot of Freud's evidence came from case studies
and it is hard to be sure about the evidence from
these as they are single individuals and everyone
is unlikely to have the same repressed emotions. ✔
Also, in case studies the analyst has to interpret
what the patient says and this process is subjective –
a different analyst might come up with a different
explanation. ✔   **[4]**

(May 2004)

Each of these points is correct and thorough but the candidate
had missed one mark. This could have been gained by: using
further evidence such as supporting case studies, by explaining
that it is difficult to distinguish between ordinary forgetting
and the effect of defence mechanisms, or by elaborating
on why/how the Adams study was well controlled.

Question 5

Discuss **one** physiological theory of dreaming.

Hobson & McCarley suggested that we dream
because our brains are randomly activated during
sleep. ✔ **(AO1)** *This starts in the brain stem then*
spreads to areas responsible for vision, movement
and sounds. ✔ **(AO1)** *There is evidence to support*
this idea from electrical recordings of PGO waves
which start from cells in the pons that start firing
randomly when dreaming begins. ✔ **(AO2)**
The brain interprets the random messages and
uses memories to make sense of them to make up
a story. ✔ **(AO1)** *This is called synthesis and*
produces what we recall as a dream. ✔ **(AO1)**
It is a good theory because it can account for why
dreams are a bit bizarre – because the activation
is random ✔ **(AO2)** *but also why they seem to make*
sense (because of the synthesis process that fits the
random ideas together sensibly). ✔ **(AO2)** *But this*
can't be entirely right because if the activation
was always random we would dream something
different every night but we don't, some people
have recurring dreams. ✔ **(AO2)**   **[12]**

(May 2004)

This is a concise, well written answer. The level of detail
about the theory is good and the evaluation is appropriate.
Note that, even though activation-synthesis is quite a technical
idea, the answer does not have to be very biological to gain
full marks. This was an essay-style question so marks are also
awarded for the quality of the written work. The candidate
uses term such as 'activation' and 'synthesis' appropriately
and the spelling and grammar are good so they would
gain both of the two marks for *clarity and communication*.
There is sufficient depth and a good balance between
description (AO1) and commentary/evaluation (AO2) and
between strengths and weaknesses. This answer therefore
also earns 2 marks for *balance and breadth*.

assessment objectives revisited

You would not be given information about the assessment objective being tested by each question in an examination, but it is worth being aware – as described in the Introduction – of which kinds of questions are asking for AO1 and which for AO2. The table below indicates the marks per topic and question relating to each Assessment Objective. Remember that the questions discussed in this chapter do not form whole papers but are a selection of questions. In an actual paper, 40 marks are for AO1 and 32 for AO2.

question number	approach	target of question	number of marks	assessment objective
unit 1				
1	cognitive-developmental	methods	3	AO1
2	cognitive	general assumptions	3	AO1
3 (a)	social	general assumptions	3	AO1
3 (b)	social	studies	2	AO1
3 (c)	social	studies	4	AO2
4 (a)	social	theories	6	AO1
4 (b)	social	theories	4	AO2
4 (c)	social	application	6	AO1
5	cognitive	contemporary issue	3	AO1
5	cognitive	contemporary issue	6	AO2
total			**40**	**26 AO1** (65%)
				14 AO2 (35%)
unit 2				
1	physiological	in-depth area of knowledge	3	AO1
2 (a)	learning	in-depth area of knowledge	3	AO1
2 (b)	learning	research method	8	AO2
3	learning	application	5	AO1
4 (a), (b), (c)	psychodynamic	in-depth area of knowledge	9	AO1
4 (d)	psychodynamic	theory	4	AO2
5	physiological	theory	6	AO1
5	physiological	theory	6	AO2
total			**44**	**26 AO1** (60%)
				18 AO2 (40%)

Abernethy, E.M. (1940) The effect of changed environmental conditions upon the results of college examinations. *Journal of Psychology*, **10**, 293–301.

Adams, H.E., Wright, L.W. and Lohr, B.A. (1996) Is homophobia associated with homosexual arousal? *Journal of Abnormal Psychology*, **105** (3), 440–5.

Aggleton, J.P. and Waskett, L. (1999) The ability of odours to serve as state-dependent cues for real-world memories: Can Viking smells aid the recall of Viking experiences? *British Journal of Psychology*, **90**, 1–7.

Aronson, E., Wilson, T.D. and Akert, R.M. (1994) *Social Psychology*. New York: Harper Collins.

Aserinsky, E. and Kleitman, N. (1953) Regularly occurring periods of eye motility and concomitant phenomena during sleep. *Science*, **118**, 273–4.

Atkinson, R.E. and Shiffrin, R.M. (1968) Human memory: A proposed system and its control processes. In Spence, K.W. and Spence, J.T. (eds) *The Psychology of Learning and Motivation*, Vol. 2. London: Academic Press.

Ayllon, T. and Azrin, N.H. (1968) *The Token Economy: A Motivated System for Therapy and Rehabilitation*. New York: Appleton-Century Crofts.

Baillargeon, R. and DeVos, J. (1991) Object permanence in young infants: further evidence. *Child Development*, **62**, 1227–46.

Bandura, A. (1977) *Social Learning Theory*. Englewood Cliffs, NJ: Prentice-Hall.

Bandura, A., Ross, D. and Ross, S.A. (1961) Transmission of aggression through imitation of aggressive models. *Journal of Abnormal and Social Psychology*, **63**, 575–82.

Bandura, A., Ross, D. and Ross, S.A. (1963) Imitation of film-mediated aggressive models. *Journal of Abnormal and Social Psychology*, **66**, 3–11.

Berson, Y., Shamir, B., Avolio, B.J. and Popper, M. (2001) The relationship between vision strength, leadership style and context. *Leadership Quarterly*, **12**, 53–73.

Blagrove, M. and Hartnell, S.J. (2000) Lucid dreaming: associations with internal locus of control, need for cognition and creativity. *Personality and Individual Differences*, **28** (1), 41–7.

Blass, T. (1996) Attribution of responsibility and trust in the Milgram obedience experiment. *Journal of Applied Social Psychology*, **26**, 1529–35.

Bohannon, J.N. (1988) Flashbulb memories for the space shuttle disaster: a tale of two theories. *Cognition*, **29**, 179–96.

Bohannon, J.N. and Symons, L.V. (1992) Flashbulb memories: confidence, consistency, and quantity. In Wingograd, E. and Neisser, U. (eds) *Affect and Accuracy in Recall: Studies of 'Flashbulb' Memories* (pp 65–91). Cambridge: Cambridge University Press.

Bornas, X. and Llabres, J. (2001) Helping students build knowledge: what computers should do. *Information Technology in Childhood Education Annual*, **13**, 267–80.

Bowen, A.M. and Bourgeouis, M.J. (2001) Attitudes towards lesbian, gay and bisexual college students: the contribution of pluralistic ignorance, dynamic social impact and contact theories. *Journal of American College Health*, **50**, 91–6.

Bradmetz, J. (1999) Precursors of formal thought: a longitudinal study. *British Journal of Developmental Psychology*, **17**, 61–81.

Bransford, J.D., Franks, J.J., Morris, C.D. and Stein, B.S. (1979) Some general constraints on learning and memory research. In Cermak, L.S. and Craik, F.I.M. (eds) *Levels of Processing in Human Memory*. Hillsdale, NJ: Lawrence Erlbaum Associates Inc.

Brown, G.W. and Harris, T. (1978) *The Social Origins of Depression: A Study of Psychiatric Disorder in Women*. London: Tavistock.

Brown, R. and Kulik, J. (1977) Flashbulb memories. *Cognition*, **5**, 73–99.

Brylowski, A. (1990) Nightmares in crisis: clinical applications of lucid dreaming techniques. *Psychiatric Journal of the University of Ottowa*, **15** (2): 79–84.

Burns, A. (1998) 'Pop' psychology or 'Ken behaving badly'. *The Psychologist*, **11** (7), 360.

Charlton, T., Gunter, B. and Hannan, A. (eds) (2000) *Broadcast Television Effects in a Remote Community*. Mahwah, NJ: Lawrence Erlbaum Associates.

Chernulnik, P.D., Donley, K.A., Wiewel, T.S.R. and Miller, S. (2001) Charisma is contagious: the effect of leaders' charisma on observers' affect.

Journal of Applied Social Psychology, **31**, 2149–59.

Craik, F.I.M. and Lockhart, R.S. (1972) Levels of processing: a framework for memory research. *Journal of Verbal Learning and Verbal Behaviour*, **11**, 671–84.

Craik, F.I.M. and Tulving, E. (1975) Depth of processing and retention of words in episodic memory. *Journal of Experimental Psychology: General*, **104**, 268–94.

Crook, C. (1994) *Computers and the Collaborative Experience of Learning*. London: Routledge.

Davidson, P.S.R. and Glisky, E.L. (2002) Is flashbulb memory a special instance of source memory? Evidence from older adults. *Memory*, **10**, 99–111.

Dement, W.C. and Kleitman, N. (1957) The relation of eye movements during sleep to dream activity: an objective method for the study of dreaming. *Journal of Experimental Psychology*, **53**, 339–46.

Deutsch, M. and Collins, M.E. (1951) *Interracial Housing*. Minneapolis: University of Florida Press.

Dobbs, M. and Crano, W.D. (2001) Outgroup accountability in the minimal group paradigm: implications for aversive discrimination and social identity theory. *Personality & Social Psychology Bulletin*, **27**, 355–64.

Duka, T., Weissenborn, R. and Dienes, Z. (2001) State-dependent effects of alcohol on recollective experience, familiarity and awareness on memories. *Psychopharmacology*, **153**, 295–306.

Duker, P.C. and Seys, D.M. (2000) A quasi-experimental study on the effect of electrical aversion treatment on imposed mechanical restraint for severe self-injurious behaviour. *Research in Developmental Disabilities*, **21**, 235–42.

Eley, T.C. and Stevenson, J. (2000) Specific life-events and chronic experiences differentially associated with depression and anxiety in young twins. *Journal of Abnormal Child Psychology*, **28**, 383–94.

Emmelkamp, P.M. (1994) Behaviour therapy with adults. In Bergin, A.E. and Garfield, S.L. (eds) (1994) *Handbook of Psychotherapy and Behaviour Change*. New York: Wiley.

Eng, L. (1995) Internet is becoming a very useful tool for campus radicals. *The Journal Star*, 22 Jan, 8.

Erikson, E.H. (1959) *Identity and the Lifecycle*. New York: Norton.

Eron, L.D. (1995) Media violence: how it affects kids and what can be done about it. Invited address presented at the annual meeting of the American Psychological Association, New York.

Eron, L.D., Huesmann, L.R., Leftowitz, M.M. and Walder, L.O. (1972) Does television violence cause aggression? *American Psychologist*, **27**, 253–63.

Eron, L.D. and Huesmann, L.R. (1986) The role of television in the development of antisocial and prosocial behavior. In Olweus, D., Block, J. and Radke-Yarrom, M. (eds) *Development of Antisocial and Prosocial Behaviour: Theories and Issues*. New York: Academic Press.

Facer, K., Furlong, J., Furlong, R. and Sutherland, R. (2003) *ScreenPlay: Children and Computing in the Home*. London: Routledge.

Folkard, S. (1996) Bags of time to play. *Daily Express*, 28 September 1996.

Foot, H., Morgan, M. and Shute, R. (eds) (1990) *Children Helping Children*. Chichester: Wiley.

Forde, E.M.E. and Humphreys, G.W. (2002) The role of semantic knowledge in short-term memory. *Neurocase*, **8**, 13–27.

Freud, S. (1894) The defence neuropsychoses. *Collected Papers Volume 1*, 59–75. London: Hogarth Press.

Freud, S. (1900) *The Interpretation of Dreams*. London: Hogarth.

Freud, S. (1905) *Three Essays on Sexuality*. London: Hogarth.

Gaertner, S.L., Mann, J.A., Murrell, A.J. and Dovidio, J.E. (1989) Reducing inter-group bias: the benefits of recategorisation. *Journal of Personality and Social Psychology*, **57**, 239–49.

Gaertner, S.L., Mann, J.A., Dovidio, J.E., Murrell, A.J. and Pomare, M. (1990) How does cooperation reduce intergroup bias? *Journal of Personality and Social Psychology*, **59**, 692–704.

Geyer, A.L.J. and Steyrer, J.M. (1998) Transformational leadership and objective performance in banks, *Applied Psychology: An International Review*, **47** (3), 397–420.

Glanzer, M. and Cunitz, A.R. (1966) Two storage mechanisms in free recall. *Journal of Verbal Learning and Verbal Behaviour*, **5**, 351–60.

Godden, D. and Baddeley, A.D. (1975) Context dependent memory in two natural environments: On land and under water. *British Journal of Psychology*, **66**, 325–31.

Golombok, S. (2000) *Parenting: What Really Counts?* London: Routledge.

Green, C. and McCreery, C. (1994) *Lucid Dreaming: The Paradox of Consciousness During Sleep*. London: Routledge.

Hagell, A. and Newbury, T. (1994) *Young Offenders and the Media*, London: Policy Studies Institute.

Harma, M., Suvanto, S. and Partinen, M. (1994) The effect of four-day round trip flights over 10 time zones on the sleep-wakefulness of airline flight attendants. *Ergonomics*, **37** (9), 1462–78.

Herxheimer, A. and Petrie, K.J. (2001) Melatonin for preventing and treating jet lag. *Cochrane Database for Systemic Reviews*, **1**, CD001520.

Heston, L.L. (1966) Psychiatric disorders in foster home reared children of schizophrenic mothers. *British Journal of Psychiatry*, **112**, 819–25.

Hobson, J.A. and McCarley, R.W. (1977) The brain as a dream state generator: an activation-synthesis hypothesis of the dream process, *American Journal of Psychiatry*, **134**, 1335–48.

Hofling, K.C., Brotzman, E., Dalrymple, S., Graves, N. and Pierce, C.M. (1966) An experimental study in the nurse-physician relationship. *Journal of Nervous and Mental Disorders*, **143**, 171–80.

Holloway, S. and Valentine, V. (2003) *Cyberkids: Children in the Information Age*. London: Routledge.

House, R.J., Spangler, W.D. and Woycke, J. (1991) Personality and charisma in the US presidency: a psychological theory of leader effectiveness. *Administrative Science Quarterly*, **36**, 364–96.

Hughes, M. (1975) *Egocentrism in Preschool Children*. Ph.D. thesis, Edinburgh University.

Jerabek, I. and Standing, L. (1992) Imagined test situations produce contextual memory enhancement. *Perceptual and Motor Skills*, **75**, 400.

Joy, L.A., Kimball, M.M. and Zabrack, M.L. (1986) Television and children's aggressive behavior. In Williams, T.M. (ed.) *The Impact of Television: A Natural Experiment in Three Communities* (pp 303–60). Orlando, FL: Academic Press.

Kiesler, S., Siegel, J. and McGuire, T.W. (1984) Social-psychological aspects of computer-mediated interaction. *American Psychologist*, **39**, 1123–34.

Koehler, T., Thiede, G. and Thoens, M. (2002) Long and short-term forgetting of word associations: an experimental study of the Freudian concepts of resistance and repression. *Zeitschrift fuer Klinishe Psychologie, Psychiatrie und Psychotherapie*, **50**, 328–33.

Krackow, A. and Blass, T. (1995) When nurses obey or defy inappropriate physician orders: attributional differences. *Journal of Social Behaviour & Personality*, **10**, 585–94.

La Berge, S.P., Nagel, L.E., Dement, W.C. and Zarcone, V.P. (1981) Lucid dreaming verified by volitional communication during REM sleep. *Perceptual and Motor Skills*, **52**, 727–32.

Lamb, M. (1998) Cybersex: research notes on the characteristics of visitors to online chatrooms. *Deviant Behaviour: An Interdisciplinary Journal*, **19**, 121–35.

Lemma-Wright, A. (1995) *Invitation to Psychodynamic Psychology*. London: Whurr.

Li, C.N., Nuttall, R.L. and Zhao, S. (1999) A test of the Piagetian water-level task with Chinese students. *Journal of Genetic Psychology*, **160**, 369–80.

Lou, Y., Abrami, P.C. and d'Apollonia, S. (2001) Small group and individual learning with technology: a meta-analysis. *Review of Educational Research*, **71**, 449–521.

Maguire, E.A., Frackowiak, R.S.J. and Frith, C.D. (1997) Recalling routes around London: activation of the right hippocampus in taxi drivers. *Journal of Neuroscience*, **17**, 7103.

McAdams, D.P., Diamond, A. and St Aubin, A. (1997) Stories of commitment: the psychosocial construction of generative lives. *Journal of Personality & Social Psychology*, **72**, 678–94.

McCafferty, S. (2002) Gesture and creating zones of proximal development for second language learning. *The Modern Language Journal*, **86** (2), 192–203.

McGarrigle, J. and Donaldson, M. (1974) Conservation accidents. *Cognition*, **3**, 341–50.

Meadows, S. (1995) Cognitive development. In Bryant, P.E. and Colman, A.M. (eds) *Developmental Psychology*. London: Longman.

Meddis, R. (1977) *The Sleep Instinct*. London: Routledge & Kegan Paul.

Mevarech, Z., Silber, O. and Fine, D. (1991) Learning with computers in small groups: cognitive and affective outcomes. *Journal of Educational Computing Research*, **7** (2), 233–43.

Mickelson, K.D. (1997) Seeking social support: parents in electronic support groups. In Kiesler, S. (ed.) *Culture of the Internet*. Mahwah, NJ: Lawrence Erlbaum Associates.

Milavsky, J.R., Kessler, R.C., Stripp, H. and Rubens, W.S. (1982) *Television Aggression: A Panel Study*. New York: Academic Press.

Milgram, S. (1963) Behavioural study of obedience. *Journal of Abnormal and Social Psychology*, **67**, 371–8.

Milgram, S. (1974) *Obedience to Authority*. New York: Harper & Row.

Myers, L.B. and Brewin, C.R. (1994) Recall of early experience and the repressive coping style. *Journal of Abnormal Psychology*, **103** (2), 288–92.

Neisser, U. and Harsch, N. (1992) Phantom flashbulbs: false recollections of hearing the news about Challenger. In Winograd, E. and Neisser, U. (eds) op. cit.

Nordhielm, C.L. (1994) A levels of processing model of advertising repetition effects. In Scott, L.M. and Batra, R. (eds) *Persuasive Imagery: A Consumer Response Perspective*. Mahwah, NJ: Lawrence Erlbaum Associates.

Nyberg, L. (2002) Levels of processing: a view from functional brain imaging. *Memory*, **10**, 345–8.

Ohman, A., Fredrikson, M., Hugdahl, K. and Rimmo, P. (1976) The premise of equipotentiality in human classical conditioning: conditioned electrodermal responses to potentially phobic stimuli. *Journal of Experimental Psychology: General*, **105**, 313–17.

Oley N (2002) Extra credit and peer tutoring: impact on the quality of writing in introductory psychology in an open admissions college. In Griggs, R.A. (ed.) *Handbook for Teaching Introductory Psychology*, Vol. 3. Mahwah, NJ: Lawrence Erlbaum Associates.

O'Neill, R.M., Greenberg, R.P. and Fisher, S. (1992) Humour and anality. *Humour: International Journal of Humour Research*, **5**, 283–91.

Oswald, I. (1969) Human brain protein, drugs and dreams. *Nature*, **223**, 893–7.

Papert, S. (1980) *Mindstorms: Children, Computers, and Powerful Ideas*. New York: Basic Books.

Parker, I. (1999) Tracing therapeutic discourse in material culture. *British Journal of Medical Psychology*, **72**, 577–89.

Pavlov, I.P. (1927) *Conditioned Reflexes*. Oxford: Oxford University Press.

Piaget, J. and Inhelder, B. (1956) *The Child's Conception of Space*. London: Routledge & Kegan Paul.

Platow, M.J., McClinktock, C.G. and Liebrand, W.B.G. (1990) Predicting intergroup fairness and ingroup bias in the minimal group paradigm: an evaluation of three alternative paradigms. *European Journal of Social Psychology*, **20**, 221–39.

Poppe, E. and Linssen, H. (1999) In-group favouritism and the reflection of realistic dimensions of difference between national states in Central and Eastern European nationality stereotypes. *British Journal of Psychology*, **38**, 85–102.

Prior, S.M. and Welling, K.A. (2001) 'Read in your head': A Vygotskian analysis of the transition from oral to silent reading. *Reading Psychology*, **22**, 1–15.

Ralph, M.R., Foster, T.G., Davis, F.C. and Menaker, M. (1990) Transplanted suprachiasmatic nucleus determines circadian rhythm. *Science*, **247**, 975–8.

Rank, S.G. and Jacobson, C.K. (1975) Hospital nurses' compliance with medication overdose orders: a failure to replicate. *Journal of Health and Social Behaviour*, **18** (2), 188–93.

Reber, R., Perrig, W.J., Flammer, A. and Walter, D. (1994) Levels of processing and memory for emotional words. *Schweizerische Zeitschrift fuer Psychologie*, **53**, 78–85.

Rechtschaffen, A., Gilliland, M.A., Bergmann, B.M. and Winter, J.B. (1983) Physiological correlates of prolonged sleep deprivation in rats. *Science*, **221**, 182–4.

Riding, R. and Rayner, S. (1998) *Cognitive Styles and Learning Strategies*. London: Fulton.

Roazzi, A. and Bryant, P. (1998) The effect of symmetrical and asymmetrical social interaction on children as logical inference. *British Journal of Developmental Psychology*, **16**, 175–81.

Salois, K.A.N. (1999) A comparative study of the Wechsler Intelligence Scale for children 3rd edition (WISC III) test performance: Northern Cheyenne and Blackfeet Reservation Indian children with the standardisation sample. *Dissertation Abstracts International*, **60**, 1909.

Samuel, J. and Bryant, P. (1984) Asking only one question in the conservation experiment. *Journal of Child Psychology and Psychiatry*, **25**, 315–18.

Sandell, R. (1999) Long-term findings of the Stockholm Outcome of Psychotherapy and Psychoanalysis Project (STOPP). Paper presented at the Psychoanalytic long-term treatments: a challenge for clinical and empirical research in psychoanalysis meeting, Hamburg.

Schlozman, S.C. (2000) Vampires and those who slay them: using the television programme Buffy the vampire slayer in adolescent therapy and psychodynamic education. *Academic Psychiatry*, **24**, 49–54.

Scoville, W.B. and Milner, B. (1957) The loss of recent memory after bilateral hippocampal lesions. *Journal of Neurology, Neurosurgery and Psychiatry*, **20**, 11–21.

Seitz, K. and Schumann-Hengsteler, R. (2000) Mental multiplication and working memory. *European Journal of Cognitive Psychology*, **12**, 552–70.

Skal, D.J. (1993) *The Monster Show: A Cultural History of Horror*. New York: Penguin Books.

Skinner, B.E. (1948) Superstition in the pigeon. *Journal of Experimental Psychology*, **38**, 168–72.

Skinner, B.E. (1957) *Verbal Behavior*. New York: Prentice-Hall.

Solms, M. (2000) Freudian dream theory today. *The Psychologist*, **13**, 618–19.

Sonstroem, A.M. (1966) On the conservation of solids. In Bruner, J.S., Olver, R.R. and Greenfield, M. (1966) *Studies in Cognitive Growth*. New York: Wiley.

Taffinder, N.J., McManus, I.C., Gul, Y., Russell, R.C.G. and Darzi, A. (1998) Effect of sleep deprivation on surgeon's dexterity on laparoscopy simulator. *The Lancet*, **352**, 1191.

Tajfel, H. (1970) Experiments in intergroup discrimination. *Scientific American*, **223**, 96–102.

Tajfel, H. and Turner, J.C. (1979) An integrative theory of intergroup conflict. In Austin, W.G. and Worchel, S. (eds) *The Social Psychology of Intergroup Relations*. Cambridge: Cambridge University Press.

Tarnow, E. (2000) Self-destructive obedience in the airplane cockpit and the concept of obedience optimisation. In Blass, T. (ed.) *Obedience to Authority*. Mahwah, NJ: Lawrence Erlbaum Associates.

Tienari, P. (1992) Implications of adoption studies on schizophrenia. *British Journal of Psychiatry*, **161**, 52–8.

Troseth, G.L. (2003) Two-year-old children learn to use video as a source of information. *Developmental Psychology*, **39** (1), 140–50.

Tulving, E. (1972) Episodic and semantic memory. In Tulving, E. and Donaldson, W. (eds) *Organisation of Memory*. London: Academic Press.

Vidal-Vazquez, M.A. and Clemente-Diaz, M. (2000) The attraction of media violence. *PSICO*, **31** (2), 49–80.

Walker, W.R., Vogl, R.J. and Thompson, C.P. (1997) Autobiographical memory: unpleasantness fades faster than pleasantness over time. *Applied Cognitive Psychology*, **11**, 399–413.

Wallace, P. (1999) *The Psychology of the Internet*. Cambridge: Cambridge University Press.

Walther, J.B. (1993) Impression development in computer-mediated interaction. *Western Journal of Communication*, **57**, 381–98.

Watson, J.B. and Rayner, R. (1920) Conditioned emotional responses. *Journal of Experimental Psychology*, **3** (1), 1–14.

Wertsch, J.Y. (1991) *Voices of the Mind: A Sociocultural Approach to Mediated Action*. Cambridge: Harvard University Press.

Wilberg, S. (2002) Preschooler's cognitive representations of their homeland. *British Journal of Developmental Psychology*, **20**, 157–70.

Wood, D. (1991) *How Children Think and Learn*. Oxford: Blackwell.

Zinbarg, R.E., Barlow, D.H., Brown, T.A. and Hertz, R.M. (1992) Cognitive behavioural approaches to the nature and treatment of anxiety disorders. *Annual Review of Psychology*, **43**, 235–67.

A

Abernethy 17
Accessibility failure 17
Accommodation 28
Activation 70
Activation-synthesis theory 70, 76
Adams et al. 56
Adaptation 28
Adolescence 59
Adoption
    and schizophrenia 73
Adoption studies 72
Adulthood 59
Affective elements of prejudice 5
Age 48
Agency theory 4
    agentic state 4
    autonomous state 4
Agentic state 4
Aggleton & Waskett 14, 17, 18
Alex, case study 61
Anal stage 56, 57, 61
Analyse x
Analysis of symbols 54, 60
Animal learning studies 46
    worked example 93-4
Animism 28
Anxiety hierarchy 41
AO1 (Assessment Objective1) v, 96
AO2 (Assessment Objective 2) v, 96
Application 83
Apply 84
Aserinsky & Kleitman 68
Assess 84
Assessment Objectives (AO) v
    revisited 96
Assimilation 28
ATP 69
Attention 44, 48
Autonomous state 4
Availability failure 17
Aversion therapy 47

B

Baillargeon & DeVos 26, 29
Bandura 44, 48
Bandura et al. 45, 48
Bandura, Ross & Ross 38, 44
Behaviour modification 47
    worked examples 94
Behaviour therapy 47
Behavioural elements of prejudice 5
Behaviourism 15
Berson et al. 4
Biological cycles 74
    circadian rhythms 74
    infradian rhythms 74
    ultradian rhythms 74
Biological instincts 55
Blass 4
Bobo doll study 44, 45, 48

Bohannon 21
Bohannon & Symons 21
Bornas & Labres 34
Bottom-up processing 15
Bowen & Bourgeois 9
Bradmetz 29
Brain, studying 71
    CAT 71
    EEG 71
    Lesioning 71
    MRI 71
    PET 71
    scanning 71
Brain-damaged patients 19
Brain wave patterns 68
Bransford 16
Brown & Harris 61
Brown & Kulik 21
Buffy, psychodynamic approach 62

C

Capacity, of memory 16
Case studies 19, 54
    of brain-damaged patients 19
    people in therapy 60
CAT (Computerised
    axial tomography) 71
Challenger space shuttle explosion,
    flashbulb memory 21
Charismatic leadership 4
    and personal characteristics 4
    and social processes 4
Charlton et al. 48
Chernulnik et al. 4
Child-centred learning 33
Childhood 53, 59
Children
    and Internet risk 10
Circadian rhythms 74
    melatonin 74
    pineal gland 74
    SCN (Suprachiasmatic nucleus) 74
Classical conditioning
    and anxiety hierarchy 41
    aversion therapy 47
    behaviour therapy 47
    mechanisms of 40
    and one trial learning 41
    and phobias 41
    and preparedness 41
    systematic desensitisation 41, 47
    worked example 93
Clinical interviews 54, 60
Closed questions 8
Cognition 27
    decentration 27
    worked example 92-3
Cognitive abilities
    nature 27
    nurture 27
    reflexes 27

    schemata 27
Cognitive elements of prejudice 5
Cognitive interviews 20
Collective action 9, 10
    and Islamic culture 10
    and social identification 10
    and Tiananmen Square 10
Compare 84
Comparison 9
Computer analogy 15
    worked example 90
Computers in education
    Bornas & Labres 34
    discovery learning 34
    Lou et al. 34
    Mevarech et al. 34
    Papert 34
    Piaget 34
    scaffolding 34
    theory of cognitive
        development 34
    Vygotsky 34
Computerised
    axial tomography (CAT) 71
Concrete operational stage 28, 33
Condensation 58
Conditioned response (CR) 40
Conditioned stimulus (CS) 40
Conscious mind 55
Conservation experiments 28, 29
Conservation of liquid 28
Conservation of number 28, 29
Contemporary issues
    how are they tested? ix
    what are they? ix
Context cues 17, 20
Context dependent forgetting 17
Continuous reinforcement 42
Contrast 84
Co-operation 9
Co-operative group work 33
Craik & Tulving 14, 16, 18
Cue dependency 17, 20, 21
    and context cues 17, 20
    and context dependent
        forgetting 17
    and state cues 17, 20
Culture, influence of 3

D

Davidson & Glisky 21
Decay theory 20, 21
Decentration 27
Deep processing 16, 83
Defence mechanisms 54, 62
    worked examples 95
Define 84
Dement and Kleitman 73
Denial 56
Dependent variable 46
Describe 84
Desynchronisation 75

Deutsch & Collins 9
Discourse analysis
    and prejudice 5
Discovery learning 33, 34
Discrimination 5, 39
Discriminatory responses 9
Discursive theory 5, 9
    and discourse analysis 5
    and language 5
Discuss 84
Disequilibrium 28
Displacement 56, 58
Distinguish 84
Divers study 17
Dizygotic twins 72
Dobbs & Crano 5
Dogs, Pavlov's 40
Dream theory 58
    condensation 58
    displacement 58
    latent content 58
    manifest content 58
    secondary elaboration 58
Dreaming 70
    activation-synthesis
        model of 70, 76
    case studies 54
    clinical interviews 54
    lucid 76
    reorganisational theory of 75, 76
    worked example 94, 95
Duka et al. 17
Duker & Seys 47
Duration, of memory 16

E

Early childhood 54
Early experience, importance of 53
Ecological theory of sleep 76
Ecological validity
    and field experiments 8
Education 33
    child-centred learning 33
    concrete operational stage 33
    co-operative group work 33
    discovery learning 33
    formal operational thinking
        stage 33
    individual learning plans 33
    national curriculum 33
    peer tutoring 33
    pre-operational stage 33
    readiness approach 33
    scaffolding 33
    Vygotsky 33
    ZPD 33
EEG (Electroencephalogram) 68, 71, 76
Ego 54, 55
Egocentricity 28, 29
Electra complex 54
Electric shocks, Milgram 6

index

Electroencephalogram (EEG) 71
Electromyogram 68
Electrooculogram (EOG) 68, 76
Eley & Stevenson 61
Emmelkamp 41
Encoding, memory 16
Endogenous (internal) rhythm 75
Endogenous pacemakers 74
Environment, importance of 39
EOG (Electrooculogram) 68, 76
Equal status contact 9
    and the Internet 10
Equilibrium 28
Erikson 62
    and mental health 61
    psychosocial stages 59
    theory of lifespan development 59
Eron 48
Eron et al. 48
Eron & Huesmann 48
Ethics xi
Evaluate x, 84
Evaluating studies x
Evaluating theories xii
Evolutionary theory 69
Exam note 70
    learning approach 41, 43, 45
    physiological approach 70
    social approach 3
Exam questions, terms 84
Exam technique 80, 84
Experiments 19
    independent measures design 19
    repeated measures design 19
Expertism 10
Explain 84
Extinction 39, 42
Eyewitness testimony
    and cue-dependency 20
    and decay theory 20
    and multistore model 20

F
Facer et al. 10
Field experiments 8
Fixed interval reinforcement 42
Fixed ratio reinforcement 42
'FK', study of 16
Flashbulb memories
    cue dependency 21
    decay theory 21
    levels of processing 21
    long-term memory 21
    multistore model 21
Folkard 75
Foot et al. 33
Forde & Humphreys 16
Forgetting 17
    and divers study 17
    and smelly museum study 17, 18
Formal operational thinking stage 28,

29, 33
Freud 17, 55, 62
    analysis of symbols 60
    clinical interviews 60
    defence mechanisms 54, 56
    dream theory 54, 58
    ego 54, 55
    id 54, 55
    levels of consciousness 55
    and Little Hans 57
    and mental health 54, 61
    oral stage 56
    psychosexual development 54, 56
    repressed memories 54
    research methods 60
    structural models 55
    superego 54, 55
    topographical studies 55
    unconscious mind 54
    worked example 94

G
Gender 48
General assumptions
    cognitive approach 14, 15
    cognitive-developmental
        approach 26, 27
    how are they tested? vi
    learning approach 38, 39
    physiological approach 66, 67
    psychodynamic approach 52, 53
    social approach 2, 3
    what are they? vi
Generalisation 39
Genetic influences, importance of 67
Genetics, studying 72
    adoption studies 72
    twin studies 72
Geniculate nucleus 70
Genital 57
Geyer & Steyrer 4
Godden & Baddeley 17
Groups, influence of 3
Growth hormone 69

H
Hagell and Newbury 48
Harma et al. 75
'Herman the Cat' 45
Heston 73
'HM', study of 16
Hobson & McCarley 58, 70
Hofling et al. 2, 7
Holloway & Valentine 10
House et al. 4
Hughes 29

I
Id 53, 54, 55
Identification 9
Identify 84

Identity versus role confusion 62
Illustrate x
Imitation 44, 48
    age 48
    gender 48
    personality 48
    power 48
    status 48
Independent measures design 19, 46
Independent variable 46
In-depth areas of study
    how are they tested? vii
    what are they? vii
Individual learning plans 33
Individuals, influence of 3
Infancy 59
Information processing approach 15
    and behaviourism 15
    bottom-up processing 15
    top-down processing 15
Infradian rhythms 74
In-group 5
Inter-group contact 9
Internet interaction
    and collective action 10
    and reducing prejudice 10
    risk to children 10
    and social identity theory 10
    trolling 10
Inter-observer reliability 32
Islamic culture 10

J
Jerabek and Standing 17
Jet lag 75
Joy et al. 48

K
Keisler et al. 10
Key application
    cognitive approach 14, 20
    cognitive-developmental
        approach 26, 33
    how are they tested? viii
    learning approach 38, 47
    physiological approach 66, 75
    psychodynamic approach 52, 61
    social approach 2, 9
    what are they? viii
Koehler et al. 56
Krackow & Blass 7

L
La Berge et al. 76
Laboratory experiments 46, 56
    dependent variable 46
    independent measures design 46
    independent variable 46
    repeated measures design 46
Lamb 10
Language 30

and prejudice 5
and Vygotsky 31
Latency 57
Latent content 58
Leading questions 20
    and cognitive interviews 20
    and context cues 20
    and state cues 20
Learning approach
    worked example 93-4
Learning cycle 30
Learning, processes of 39
    worked examples 94
Lemma-Wright 61
Lesioning 71, 75
Levels of consciousness 55
Levels of processing
    theory (LoP) 16, 20, 21
    deep processing 16
    phonemic processing 16
    semantic processing 16
    structural processing 16
Libido 56
Little Albert 40
Little Hans 57
Long-term memory (LTM) 16, 21
Longitudinal studies 32
    worked example 90
Lou et al. 31, 34
LTM (Long-term memory) 16, 21
Lucid dreaming 76

M
Magnetic resonance imaging (MRI) 71
Maguire et al. 71
McAdams et al. 59
McCafferty 33
McGarrigle & Donaldson 29
Meddis 69
Media violence 48
    Bobo doll 48
    imitation 48
    social learning theory 48
    St Helena experiment 48
Melatonin 75
Memory
    failure of 17
    Levels of processing theory (LoP) 16
    multistore model (MSM) 16
Mental health 54, 61
    and Erikson 61
    and Freud 61
Methods
    cognitive approach 14, 19
    cognitive-developmental
        approach 26, 32
    learning approach 38, 46
    physiological approach 66, 71
    psychodynamic approach 52, 60
    social approach 2, 8
Mevarech et al. 34

Mickelson 10
Milavsky et al. 48
Milgram 2, 4
    ethics 6
    methodology 6
Minimal groups studies 5
Model 44
Monozygotic twins 72
Motivation 44, 48, 53, 80
Mr Wallace 6
MRI (Magnetic resonance imaging) 71
MSM (Multistore model of memory) 16
Multistore model of
    memory (MSM) 16, 20, 21
    and capacity 16
    and duration 16
    and encoding 16
    'FK', study of 16
    'HM', study of 16
    primacy effect 16
    recency effect 16
    sensory register 16

N
Name 84
National curriculum 33
Nature 27
Negative punishment 42
Negative reinforcement 42
Nervous system, importance of 67
Neurones 70
Neutral stimulus (NS) 40
Non-rapid-eye-movement sleep
    (nREM) 68
Nordhielm 16
nREM (Non-rapid-eye-movement
    sleep) 68
Nurses, obedience of 7
Nurture 27

O
O'Neill et al. 57
Obedience 6
    and nurses 7
    and pilots 7
    studies of 7
    theories of 4
Object permanence 28, 29
Observational learning 44
Observations 32
Occipital lobe 70
Oedipus complex 54, 57
Ohman et al. 41
Oley 33
One trial learning 41
Open questions 8
Operant conditioning
    behaviour modification 47
    extinction 42
    and language learning 43
    mechanisms of 42
    positive reinforcement 43

punishment 42
schedule of reinforcement 42
shaping 43
Skinner 42, 43
Skinner box 42
superstitious pigeons 42
token economy 47
worked example 94
Operations 28
Oral stage 56, 57, 61
Oswald 69
Out-group 5
Outline 84

P
Papert 34
Partial reinforcement 42
Pavlov 38, 40
Peer tutoring 33
Pendulum test of formal reasoning 28
Personality 48
PET (Positron emission tomography) 71
PGO wave 70
Phallic 57
Phase delay 75
Phonemic processing 16
Piaget & Inhelder 26, 28
Piaget
    accommodation 28
    adaptation 28
    animism 28
    assimilation 28
    and computers in education 34
    concrete operations 28
    conservation 28, 29
    conservation of number 29
    disequilibrium 28
    egocentricity 28, 29
    equilibrium 28
    formal operations 28
    formal reasoning 29
    object permanence 28, 29
    operations 28
    pendulum test of formal
        reasoning 28
    schemas 28
    stages of development 29
    three mountains test 28
Pilots, obedience of 7
Pineal gland 75
Platow et al. 5
Pontine reticular formation 70
Poppe & Linssen 5
Positive punishment 42
Positive reinforcement 42, 43
Positron emission tomography (PET) 71
Power 48
Preconscious mind 55
Prejudice
    affective elements 5
    behavioural elements 5

cognitive elements 5
    and discrimination 5
    theories of 5
    reducing 9, 10
    worked example 92
Pre-operational stage 33
Preparedness 41
Primacy effect 16
Princess Diana, flashbulb memory 21
Prior & Welling 31
Projection 56
Psychosexual development 54, 57
    Electra complex 54
    Oedipus complex 54, 57
Psychosocial stages 59
Puberty 59
Punishment 42

Q
Questions
    Cognitive approach 22, 23
    Cognitive-developmental
        approach 35, 36
    Learning approach 49, 50
    Physiological approach 77, 78
    Psychodynamic approach 63, 64
    Social approach 11, 12

R
Ralph et al. 75
Rank & Jacobsen 7
Rapid-eye-movement sleep (REM) 68
Reaction formation 56
Readiness approach 33
Recency effect 16
Rechtschaffen et al. 69
Reflexes 27
Regression 56
REM (Rapid-eye-movement sleep) 68,
    70, 73, 76
    worked example 93
Reorganisational theory of
    dreaming 75, 76
Repeated measures design 19, 46
Repetition 83
Repressed memories 54
    Defence mechanisms 54
    Early childhood 54
Repression 17, 20, 53, 56
Reproduction 44, 48
Research methods
    Animal learning studies 46
    how are they tested? vii
    Laboratory experiments 46
    Learning approach 46
    what are they? vii
Response bias 8
Restorational theory of sleep 69, 75, 76
Retention 44, 48
Revision checklist
    Cognitive approach 85-6

Cognitive-developmental
    approach 86
Learning approach 87
Physiological approach 88
Psychodynamic approach 87-8
Social approach 85
Revision plan 81
Revision timetable 81
Riding & Rayner 16
Roazzi & Bryant 30

S
Salois 30
Sampling bias 8
Samuel & Bryant 29
Sandell 61
Scaffolding 30, 33
    and computers in education 34
Schedule of reinforcement 42
Schemata 27-8
Schizophrenia, adoption study of 73
Schlozman 62
SCN (Suprachiasmatic nucleus) 74, 75
Scoville & Milner 16
Secondary elaboration 58
Seitz & Schumann-Hengsteler 16
Semantic processing 16
Sensory register 16
Setting
    Milgram 7
Shaping 43
Shiftwork 75
Short-term memory (STM) 16
SIT see Social Identity Theory
Skinner 38, 42
Skinner box 42
Sleep 68, 69
    ecological theory of 76
    evolutionary theory 69
    loss 75
    restorational theory of 69, 75, 76
    stages 68
    theories of 69
Smelly museum study 17, 18
Social approach
    worked example 91
Social categorisation 5, 9, 10
Social comparison 5, 10
Social desirability 8
Social identity theory 5, 9
    collective action 9
    co-operation 9
    equal status contact 9
    expertism 10
    identification 9
    in-group 5
    inter-group contact 9
    minimal groups studies 5
    out-group 5
    social categorisation 5, 9, 10
    social comparison 5, 9, 10

social identification 5, 10
social identities 10
trolling 10
worked example 91-2
Social learning theory 44, 48
  attention 48
  Bobo doll study 44, 45, 48
  'Herman the Cat' 45
  imitation 44
  model 44
  motivation 48
  reproduction 48
  retention 48
  violence 45
Solms 58
Sonstroem 31
Specification, AS v
Spontaneous recovery 39
St Helena experiment 48
Stages of development 29
State 84
State cues 17, 20
State dependent forgetting 17
Status 48
Stereotyped beliefs 9
STM (Short-term memory) 16
Structural models 55
Structural processing 16
Studies in detail
  how are they tested? viii

what are they? viii
Superego 53, 54, 55
Superstitious pigeons 42
Suprachiasmatic nucleus (SCN) 74
Surveys 8
  closed questions 8
  open questions 8
  response bias 8
  sampling bias 8
  social desirability 8
Synthesis 70
Synthesise x
Systematic desensitisation 41, 47

T
Taffinder et al. 75
Tajfel & Turner 5
Tarnow 7
Telephone orders
  Hofling 7
  Milgram 7
Theory of cognitive development 34
Theory of lifespan development 59
Therapy 76
  lucid dreaming 76
Three mountains test of egocentrism 28
Tiananmen Square 10
Time circles, revision 81
Token economy 47
Top-down 15

Topographical studies 55
Triangulation 19
Trolling 10
Troseth 48
Tulving 17
TV violence 45
Twin studies 72

U
Ultradian rhythms 68, 74
Unconditioned response (UCR) 40
Unconditioned stimulus (UCS) 40
Unconscious mind 53, 54, 55
  defence mechanisms 54
  dreams 54
  ego 54
  Id 53, 54
  mental health 54
  psychosexual development 54
  repressed memories 54
  repression 53
  superego 53, 54
Unit 1
  revision checklist 85-6
  worked examples 90-3
Unit 2
  revision checklist 87-8
  worked examples 93-5
Unresolved conflicts 62

V
Validity xi
Variable interval reinforcement 42
Variable ratio reinforcement 42
Vicarious reinforcement 44
Vidal-Vazquez & Clemente-Diaz 48
Violence 45
Vygotsky 29, 33, 34
  and language 30, 31
  and learning cycle 30
  and scaffolding 30
  Zone of Proximal Development (ZPD) 30

W
Wallace 10
Walther 10
Watson & Rayner 38, 40
White rat study 40
Wood 30
World Trade Centre attacks, flashbulb memory 21

Z
Zeitgebers 74
Zinbarg et al. 41
Zone of Proximal Development (ZPD) 30, 33